ORIZONS IN MANAGEMENT

ditor: Professor Sir Cary Cooper, *50th Anniversary Professor
nizational Psychology and Health at Alliance Manchester
School, University of Manchester, UK and President of the
d Institute of Personnel and Development and British Academy
gement*

ortant series makes a significant contribution to the development
gement thought. This field has expanded dramatically in recent
d the series provides an invaluable forum for the publication of
lity work in management science, human resource management,
ional behaviour, marketing, management information systems,
is management, business ethics, strategic management and
onal management.
ain emphasis of the series is on the development and application
riginal ideas. International in its approach, it will include some
est theoretical and empirical work from both well-established
rs and the new generation of scholars.
in the series include:

g Performance Appraisal at Work
n and Change
ziner and Edna Rabenu

Business and Leadership
nd Organisations
Alexander-Stamatios Antoniou, Cary Cooper and Caroline

k of Research on the Psychological Contract at Work
Cary Cooper and Yannick Griep

Human Capital
a Sustainable Competitive Advantage
anza and Giuseppina Simone

Strategic Human Capital

NEW F

Series
of Org
Busines
Chartei
of Man

This im
of man
years a
high-q
organiz
operati
interna
    The
of new
of the
researc
    Title

Improv
Evoluti
Aharor

Womer
Gender
Edited
Gatrel

Handb
Edited

Strateg
Creatir
Andrea

Strategic Human Capital

Creating a Sustainable Competitive Advantage

Andrea Lanza

Professor of Strategic Management and Director of the Unical Business School (UBS) and the Master in Business Administration, University of Calabria, Italy

Giuseppina Simone

Affiliate Professor of Human Resource Management, University of Calabria, Italy

NEW HORIZONS IN MANAGEMENT

 Edward Elgar
PUBLISHING

Cheltenham, UK • Northampton, MA, USA

Published by
Edward Elgar Publishing Limited
The Lypiatts
15 Lansdown Road
Cheltenham
Glos GL50 2JA
UK

Edward Elgar Publishing, Inc.
William Pratt House
9 Dewey Court
Northampton
Massachusetts 01060
USA

A catalogue record for this book
is available from the British Library

Library of Congress Control Number: 2019956750

This book is available electronically in the **Elgar**online
Business subject collection
DOI 10.4337/9781789908596

MIX
Paper from
responsible sources
FSC
www.fsc.org   FSC® C013056

ISBN 978 1 78990 858 9 (cased)
ISBN 978 1 78990 859 6 (eBook)

Printed and bound in Great Britain by TJ International Ltd, Padstow, Cornwall

Contents

Figures

Tables

Preface

THE RELEVANCE OF HUMAN CAPITAL STRATEGY

In 2002, Billy Beane, General Manager of Oakland Athletics, a team competing in Major League Baseball (MLB), assembled an underrated group of baseball players and achieved a quite surprising number of wins, although the team's manager/head coach, Art Howe, did not share this recruiting approach (Sexton & Lewis, 2003). Despite Howe's non-cooperation, Beane managed to fully integrate the newly acquired human resources into Oakland's strategies and, although they did not win the 2002 World Series, they won 20 games in a row that season, going far beyond fans' and experts' expectations.

Between 2013 and 2016, Sam Hinkie, General Manager of the Philadelphia 76ers, one of the 30 teams comprising the National Basketball Association (NBA), decided to trade his good players for future players' picks and to recruit, meanwhile, low-quality players in order to deliberately create a weak franchise and, thus, to rank in the last positions of the NBA. This left them in a very good position for the selection of the best prospects in the subsequent years, since league rules generally give the highest draft[1] picks in reverse order to the previous season's worst teams. This strategy paid off, since the Philadelphia 76ers reached the post-season's play-offs in the following years, although they have not won the championship since 1983.

These two strategies, namely, "Moneyball" and "The Process" help us to understand how an effective human capital strategy requires several ingredients to pay off, including, in particular:

- tight coordination across the macro and the meso levels of management;
- a clear vision of what the relevant human capital assets are;
- a focus on the actual relevant characteristics of human capital assets; and

- cross-level managerial cooperation, thus coping with different expectations with regard to human capital assets' integration and development.

To this end, along with the useful insights originating from the theoretical contributions and the related empirical evidence from the macro- and micro-level approaches, we also need to include the role of the meso-managerial level. Therefore, it seemed appropriate to take on the challenge of providing a conceptual framework that filled the conceptual voids in the extant approaches, meanwhile trying to solve theoretical ambiguities and empirical inconsistencies.

THE PURPOSE OF THIS BOOK

Accordingly, the purpose of this book is to provide scholars and researchers (but also managers and experts) with a useful approach for pursuing a twofold goal: (1) to understand the dynamics underpinning the link between strategic human capital and organizational performance; and (2) to clarify some theoretical ambiguities characterizing the role of strategic human capital in the quest for a sustainable competitive advantage.

More precisely, our goal is to offer a novel conceptual framework and a robust and theoretically grounded managerial tool to help organizations get the most from their most important asset – human capital – starting from the examination of recent literature on the topic. We are confident that this book will provide a heterogeneous community – such as scholars and researchers interested in managerial disciplines, managers and decision makers, consultants and practitioners from several contexts – with a state-of-the-art examination of how strategic human capital can be harnessed to allow organizations to obtain their valuable contribution in the quest for a sustainable competitive advantage.

SCOPE, AIM, AND APPROACH

Since Gary Becker's (1964) first formulation of "human capital theory," scholars from several areas of interest in the management domain have tried to take advantage of the broad scope of such theory. For example, in the strategy field, scholars have addressed the importance of human capital from different perspectives, such as knowledge (Kogut & Zander, 1992), learning (Cohen & Levinthal, 1990), competence (Leonard-Barton, 1992 [2011]) and capabilities (Teece, Pisano, &

Shuen, 1997 [2008]). Almost in parallel, in the human resources field, researchers have investigated heterogeneous issues such as the composition of the "human capital pool" (Wright, McMahan, & McWilliams, 1994), the degree of development of employees (Lepak & Snell, 1999), and the impact of human resource management on organizational performance (Becker & Gerhart, 1996). While each stream has endeavored to investigate its own specific points of interest and research questions, thus developing a quite articulated landscape of topics, on the other hand the two areas of study have evolved into two quite sharply separated domains (Wright, Coff, & Moliterno, 2014).

To bridge this separation, this book has two main objectives: (1) to provide original empirical evidence with regard to the relationship between strategic human capital and performance; and (2) to clarify some empirical and practical ambiguities concerning strategic human capital management, and offering, at the same time, a novel conceptual framework. This approach will help both scholars and practitioners to understand the message delivered through our theoretical and empirical evidence and managerial tools.

We decided to take on the challenge underpinning this volume as we believe that there is a gap in the broad literature on human capital. Indeed, despite a great number of studies both in the human resources and the strategic management fields of research (Fulmer & Ployhart, 2014; Wright et al., 2014), our understanding of the potential advantages stemming from the management of strategic human capital is hampered by either disciplinary or methodological inconsistencies. To overcome these inconsistencies, this volume focuses on the role of strategic human capital at different managerial levels, thus providing a fruitful integration of different disciplinary views of strategic human capital, meanwhile exploring new methodological issues, especially insofar as the examination of both linear and non-monotonic (quadratic) relationships between strategic human capital and firms' results is concerned. To achieve this goal, we have conducted research on the Italian "Serie A" professional football league (the highest professional level in Italy, and among the most competitive worldwide). We have tackled this issue using a replication methodology in order to clarify this major empirical ambiguity in the field. Our theoretical approach along with our main empirical evidence provide a cutting-edge examination of how and why strategic human capital at different organizational levels can be harnessed to deliver sustainable competitive advantage. In sum, our book offers a useful managerial model to help managers and decision makers get the most from their most important asset.

CONTENT OF THE BOOK

This book is organized into four chapters. In Chapter 1, "Strategic human capital at the crossroads," we examine the most recent theoretical and empirical advances in the field of strategic human capital (SHC), with a specific focus on the theoretical inconsistencies and methodological ambiguity in both the strategic management and human resources areas of study. The chapter introduces a unifying perspective on SHC management, which will be further articulated in Chapter 4 through a novel conceptual framework.

Subsequently, in Chapter 2, "Understanding and clarifying the dynamics of strategic human capital effects on performance: A quasi-replication of major literature evidence," we clarify a key area of ambiguity in the context of human capital studies – how to deal with the shared experience of skilled individuals over a prolonged period of time. Indeed, the extant research has not clarified whether the relationship between shared experience and performance is either linearly positive or non-monotonic (inverted U-shaped). We have clarified this ambiguity and also advanced a theory with respect to the relevance of specific organizational roles in the context of the analysis of this relationship.

In Chapter 3, "The effect of strategic human capital renewal on organizational results: An empirical examination in the Italian Serie A professional football league," we observe the importance of human capital renewal choices and address the effect of heterogeneous newcomers, with respect to their general/industry expertise and personal characteristics, on performance.

Finally, in Chapter 4, "Get the most from your most important asset: A conceptual and managerial model for harnessing the value of strategic human capital," we draw a set of theoretical implications from the empirical evidence reported in the previous chapters and provide a conceptual framework that is a fruitful integration of both the clarification of the inconsistencies and ambiguities discussed in Chapter 1 and the original empirical evidence reported in Chapters 2 and 3. The fresh theoretical model presented in this chapter will help scholars, as well as managers, decision makers, and experts from various fields, enrich their research and professional toolkit.

A final reflection with respect to the overall motivation of this book concerns our aim as scholars between two important disciplines to achieve a holistic conceptual framework and a unifying perspective. We hope this book achieves that aim and offers a useful conceptual framework for the vast and heterogeneous population of scholars, managers, and experts interested in organizations' most important asset.

NOTE

1. A draft is the process used to allocate certain players to teams. In a draft, teams take turns selecting from a pool of eligible players. When a team selects a player, the team receives exclusive rights to sign that player to a contract.

Andrea Lanza
Giuseppina Simone

1. Strategic human capital at the crossroads

1.1 PERSPECTIVES ON STRATEGIC HUMAN CAPITAL

Despite the almost obvious acknowledgment of the role and the relevance of human capital in the context of economic and managerial processes, there exists – according to distinguished scholars (Ployhart & Moliterno, 2011; Wright, Coff, & Moliterno, 2014) – a significant divide in the way this fundamental resource has been investigated with respect to a number of issues, such as organizational processes, knowledge development, managerial decision making, and its contribution to firms' competitive advantage.

A major limitation in the investigation of human capital is constituted by the sharp division characterizing both theoretical advances and empirical efforts concerning the level of analysis, as scholars have adopted a rather polarized model, either focusing on the micro level (e.g., the study of individual human resources traits in the context of organizational processes) or on the macro level (that is, the analysis of aggregate human capital at the firm level through the theoretical lens of competences and capabilities). This sharp divide has generated two highly segmented research domains, each characterized by specific languages, approaches, and research methods that, however, have not helped scholars and managers achieve a unifying framework with regard to the important resource that constitutes the central topic of this book – human capital.

To fill this void and to reconcile the above two approaches, we maintain that scholars should pay attention to a series of either unaddressed or overlooked issues, such as:

- the importance of a unifying framework for dealing with human capital as an organizational-level resource;

- the relevance of a meso level in human capital resource management; and
- a fine-grained understanding of the contribution of human capital to organizational performance and competitive advantage.

In this volume, we try to address these issues and take on the challenge of providing a unifying perspective on strategic human capital. We maintain that our effort represents a useful research endeavor for both the theoretical and the managerial perspectives. In particular, we suggest that human capital resources are an extremely valuable asset in the life of every type of organization and that not addressing the above issues could hamper our understanding of the actual contribution of human capital to economic and managerial processes, at different levels of analysis, because this important resource has been investigated through several different lenses. Therefore, given that the diversity of conceptual frameworks and approaches existing in the whole human capital literature – as noted in the Preface – has engendered a number of ambiguities and inconsistencies, we aim to successfully address these ambiguities and inconsistencies in this volume.

1.2   OVERCOMING THEORETICAL INCONSISTENCIES

Human resources are the main source of competitive advantage, especially in highly competitive settings, where a bundle of valuable resources becomes central to firm success (Barney, 1991; Peteraf, 1993). Given its relevance as a source of superior performance, several studies have tried to analyze antecedents, constructs, and consequences of human resources (Ployhart & Moliterno, 2011; Ployhart, Nyberg, Reilly, & Maltarich, 2014; Wright et al., 2014).

In particular, human capital theory has its roots in both economics (Becker, 1964) and psychology (Spearman, 1927) and represents one of the main approaches to the analysis of human resources as a source of superior firm performance. Management studies have recurrently drawn from this research perspective to understand the contribution of human resources at both the individual and the organizational levels.

Human resources, though, have been observed and investigated in several research fields, following different paths. For example, according to Ployhart and Moliterno (2011), in the context of management studies, two main approaches deal with human resources as a source of competitive advantage – the micro- and macro-level approaches. More precisely, research in human resources (HR), organizational behavior (OB), and industrial organizations (IO) has focused on the *micro level* through the analysis of knowledge, skills, and abilities owned by individuals, and of their link with individual-level performance (Ployhart & Moliterno, 2011; Schmidt & Hunter, 1998). On the other hand, organization and strategy fields have focused on the *macro level* by means of the analysis of knowledge, skills, and abilities aggregated at the organizational higher level, and on their contribution to competitive advantage (Barney, 1991; Penrose, 1959; Peteraf, 1993; Ployhart & Moliterno, 2011).

This difference in the level of analysis has played an important role in the theoretical development of human capital, thus affecting the comprehension of the antecedents, consequences, and dimensions of the human capital construct. These different perspectives affected, in turn, the theoretical issues of interest (such as individual conduct, HR practice, organizational behavior, and so on), research methodologies, the selection of empirical measures, and sources of data. In particular, *micro-level* studies, instead, focused mainly on the link between individual characteristics and job performance and, because individual characteristics must be measured too, reliability and construct validity are the cornerstone of methodologies adopted for this purpose. *Macro-level* studies, instead, have relied on different methodologies, mostly through an extensive use of econometrics, thus focusing on longitudinal archival data as a primary source of information (Wright et al., 2014).

However, a specific level of analysis (either at the micro or at the macro level) is doomed to lead to a partial explanation and understanding of the phenomena of interest, since those studies that adopted a micro-level approach did not consider how individual characteristics contribute to competitive advantage, while studies at the macro level neglected the analysis of the acquisition and nurturing of valuable human resources in the context of human capital generation and development, given that their focus was, mainly, on resource heterogeneity and its influence on firm performance. Furthermore, this neglect has given rise to the critique that, from the macro-level perspective, a firm is a black box (Mahoney, 1995; Priem & Butler, 2001; Van de Ven & Polley, 1992), a theoretical issue that requires a deeper understanding of resources' microfoundation. In summary, it seems that in the last three decades a quite broad divide has affected the fields of research interested in the contribution of human resources and human capital to organizational results.

To overcome this separation, a new area of interest has emerged. Defined as strategic human resource management (SHRM), its main focus is on "the pattern of planned human resource deployments and activities intended to enable the firm to achieve its goals" (Wright & McMahan, 1992, p. 298). From this viewpoint, the SHRM domain deals with "the determinants of decisions about HR practices, the composition of human capital resource pool, the specification of the required human resource behaviours, and the effectiveness of these decisions given various business strategies and/or competitive situations" (Wright & McMahan, 1992, p. 298).

Despite the breadth of the issues covered by the above statement, this approach has left some theoretical inconsistencies unaddressed, mostly because it suggested that the main purpose of SHRM research was an advance in the understanding of the link between HR practice and job performance, rather than the development of the human capital construct. This research perspective has been subsequently buttressed by empirical studies showing how HR practices positively affect firm performance (Combs, Liu, Hall, & Ketchen, 2006; Huselid, 1995). In particular, these studies focused on the development of a high-performance system that, by means of the exploitation of individual knowledge, skills, abilities, and other characteristics (KSAOs), investigate how firms achieve competitive advantage. However, the studies failed to investigate the dynamics that lead to resource creation at unit level (Ployhart & Moliterno, 2011). For example, are a unit's human resources just an aggregation of individual characteristics? This question has not been answered, yet.

In essence, because a full integration of the two research perspectives has not been reached, some issues have remained unexplored, such as the dynamics that lead to the creation of valuable resources at the firm level, a void that affects, in turn, the understanding of what should be the appropriate endowment of resources for competitive purpose. This is because micro-level studies focus on how individual characteristics affect the ability to perform a specific task and assume this ability as an antecedent of firm performance. However, this approach fails to explain how these individual characteristics interact with other human resources, culture, strategy, and experience embedded in a given firm, nor does it provide a clear examination of how middle managers interact with other human resources at the individual level. On the other hand, macro-level research focuses on higher-level dynamics based on aggregate human resources conceived of as a bundle of individuals. However, this research perspective too omits to explain how resources are shaped at higher levels, and how middle managers contribute to this purpose.

In sum, human resources available for firms' purposes are treated, in many studies, as the sum of the individual KSAOs, thus neglecting the interaction with other human resources already present and embedded in the organization. This neglect implies that the way in which both cognitive and non-cognitive levels of experience and skills are combined requires further exploration. In particular, scholars, experts, and managers are not provided with a conceptual framework for addressing their specific professional needs with respect to the consequences of many crucial decisions in the context of human resource endowment. This is because the understanding of how resources combine and aggregate within the organization, starting from the initial KSAO endowment, is still limited. More precisely, we maintain that the dynamics concerning the evolution of human resource endowment at the organizational level requires further examination with regard to, in particular, renewal choices of human capital under the specific circumstances of an organization's short- and long-term needs.

We maintain that the analysis of the interactions between renewal choices and the initial endowment of human capital can lead to an important advance in the understanding of resource development at the unit level (Kozlowski & Klein, 2000; Ployhart et al., 2014). This implies, in turn, the integration of the micro- and the macro-level approaches into a holistic research framework that includes the meso level too, in order to explain higher-order resources generation and their relationship with organizational performance.

Figure 1.1 reports the evolution of the two different research approaches so far considered, (i.e., psychology and economics perspectives), whose convergence in the SHRM framework, although useful and influential, falls far short of scholars' and managers' expectations with regard to a compelling unifying approach.

A major limitation of the convergence of the above-mentioned scholarly perspectives in the SHRM framework involves their juxtaposition, which highlights that they are not fully integrated, an occurrence that affects our comprehension of the processes regarding the acquisition, development, retention, and renewal of human resources at the organizational level. In particular, the gap between these two different perspectives points to the need to define a new research domain to overcome the above limitations and open a dialogue between their diverging topics.

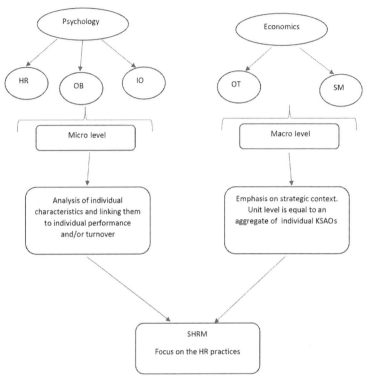

Note: HR = human resources; OB = organizational behavior; IO = industrial
organizations; OT = organizational theory; SM = strategic management.

Figure 1.1   *Human capital resource perspectives*

To this end, Wright et al. (2014) call for the development of a common
platform and identify several issues on which to build a dialogue between
these research fields. In particular, they invite convergence on a specific
set of issues, namely, how to assess and define human capital at different
levels of analysis; what are the main individual characteristics that can be
considered as human capital; why do firms choose a specific investment
in human capital instead of other types of investment; what type of human
capital is actually strategic for a given firm; what is the role played by
firm specificity on value creation; and what are the dynamics that allow
for the appropriation of the value generated by strategic human capital.

Notwithstanding the relevance of these theoretical issues, it seems that our understanding of the human capital domain is hampered by the lack of a unifying definition of its construct and of the related dimensions. For instance, while Campbell, Coff, and Kryscynski (2012) consider human capital as an employer's investment and focus on its relationship with firms' performance, Ployhart and Moliterno (2011) define human capital at unit level as an emergent phenomenon originating from individual KSAOs.

The lack of widespread acceptance of a common construct concerning human capital resources, in turn, implies that there are some basic theoretical issues requiring further conceptual investigation, namely:

- what is human capital;
- what are human capital antecedents; and
- what are the consequences of investments in human capital development.

These basic theoretical points are important because, according to Ployhart et al. (2014), there are many inconsistencies in extant studies that hamper our understanding of human capital at different levels and how it contributes to value creation at the organizational level. Table 1.1 lists the main definitions of human capital resources proposed by Ployhart et al. (2014).

The review of the main contributions on human capital proposed by Ployhart et al. (2014) highlights the absence of a shared framework concerning both the definition and the levels of analysis. This bears important implications with regard to the validity of the human capital resource construct and, in turn, with respect to our understanding of the consequences of a specific combination of resources on a firm's competitive advantage.

To fill this void, Wright et al. (2014) suggest a combination of two dimensions: (1) the level of analysis; and (2) the malleability of individual characteristics. The aim of their framework is to reach a common definition of the human capital construct. This seems a promising advance, since it takes account of the dynamic that generates an increasing value for organizations by introducing different levels of analysis and, also, the link between human resources and firm performance to achieve an advancement from both the theoretical and the empirical standpoints. More precisely, these authors suggest developing SHRM over three levels of analysis: (1) intra-individual level; (2) individual level; and (3)

Table 1.1   *Main definitions of human capital resources*

Article	Definition	Level of Analysis	Disciplinary Origin
Becker (2002, p. 3)	"Human capital refers to the knowledge, information, ideas, skills, and health of individuals"	Individual	Economics
Coff and Kryscynski (2011, p. 1430)	Human capital: "an individual's stock of knowledge, skills, and abilities"	Individual	Strategy/ microfoundations
	Firm-level human assets: "firm-level aggregation of employee skills"	Firm	Strategy
Crook, Todd, Combs, Woehr, and Ketchen (2011, p. 444)	"The term human capital refers to the knowledge, skills and abilities (KSAs) embodied in people"	Firm/ individual	Strategy
Hitt, Biermant, Shimizu, and Kochhar (2001, p. 14)	"Human capital attributes (including education, experience, and skills) . . . of top managers affect firm outcomes"	Firm	Strategy
Huselid, Jackson, and Schuler (1997, p. 171)	"Employees' collective knowledge, skills, and abilities"	Firm	Strategic human resources management
Kor and Leblebici (2005, p. 968)	"Firms' strategic human resources such as professionals with specialized knowledge and expertise"	Firm	Strategy
Ployhart and Moliterno (2011, pp. 127–128)	"A unit level resource that is created from the emergence of individuals' knowledge, skills, abilities and other characteristics (KSAOs)"	Unit	Psychology/strategy
Somaya, Williamson, and Lorinkova (2008, p. 936)	"Defined broadly as the cumulative knowledge, skills, talent, and knowhow of the firm's employees"	Firm	Strategy/ knowledge-based view

Article	Definition	Level of Analysis	Disciplinary Origin
Wright and McMahan (2011, p. 95)	"At the unit level, human capital can refer to the aggregate accumulation of individual human capital that can be combined in a way that creates value for the unit"	Unit	Strategic human resources management
Youndt and Snell (2004, p. 338)	"Human capital simply refers to individual employees' knowledge, skills, and expertise"	Individual	Strategic human resources management

Source: Ployhart et al. (2014), p. 375, Table 1.

unit level. The first level refers to knowledge, skills, abilities, and other traits (KSAOs) owned by individuals. The second level considers the investigation of the dimensions of competitive advantage in which individuals are embedded, and, thanks to which, individual characteristics become "capital" for organizations. Finally, a unit level of analysis is introduced, with the purpose of understanding when individual human capital can be conceived of as a human capital pool (Wright, McMahan, & McWilliams, 1994).

However, to conceptualize the human capital construct, it seems appropriate to account for the characteristics of individuals, since, as stated by Ployhart and Moliterno (2011), "the origins of human capital resources exist in the full range of KSAOs of employees within the unit" (p. 133). Thus, according to their view, the basic unit of analysis is an individual's KSAOs. This issue is broadly explored by the literature on HR practice with respect to selection methods whose purpose is to match candidate characteristics and company needs by means of employment tests (such as interviews and assessment procedures) with the purpose of measuring abilities, competencies, personality traits, and assessing cognitive and non-cognitive KSAOs and their fit with a company's goals and needs. Especially, with respect to cognitive KSAOs, following Ployhart and Moliterno (2011), we should consider four basic types of ability that, in general terms, reflect what people "can do":

- *General cognitive ability* (e.g., general mental ability or intelligence, or *g* [the g factor]) represents KSAOs that involve the comprehension, manipulation, retention, and creation of information (Jensen, 1998). It is relatively stable throughout adulthood and is the strongest predictor of educational and occupational outcomes (Carroll, 1993; Gottfredson, 1997; Jensen, 1998; Schmidt & Hunter, 1998).

- *Knowledge* is an understanding of principles, facts, and processes. Knowledge can range from generic to specific (e.g., knowledge of accounting to knowledge of how to use a particular firm's accounting software). It is usually clustered within domains such as those learned through formal education (e.g., accounting) and/or experience.
- *Skills* represent a capacity to learn more information or learn information more quickly (e.g., study skills, reading skills). They are tied to generic domains reflecting much of what is learned through formal education or experience (e.g., problem solving, social interactions).
- *Experience* is a multifaceted construct that reflects an opportunity to learn and transfer knowledge from generic, to job and firm specific. There are multiple types of experience (e.g., job, firm) that vary in terms of amount, time, and type (Quiñones, Ford, & Teachout, 1995). (Cited from Ployhart & Moliterno, 2011, p. 134, Table 2; original emphasis)

In addition, these authors recognize three types of non-cognitive KSAOs that refer to "will do" abilities: personality, interests, and values (Ployhart & Moliterno, 2011, 134, Table 2; original emphasis):

- *Personality* refers to a set of traits, generally stable throughout adulthood, that direct and maintain consistency in behavior. The Five Factor Model (FFM) of personality (McCrae & Costa, 1996) is dominant and includes *emotional stability* (resistance to anxiety and stress), *extroversion* (dominance, social striving), *openness to experience* (desire to learn and experience new things), *agreeableness* (empathy and desire to get along with others), and *conscientiousness* (dependability, achievement, reliability).
- *Interests and values* are stable throughout adulthood and represent an individual's preferences for certain types of work. The best example of this individual-level noncognitive attribute is Holland's RIASEC[1] model (1997), which notes that people choose occupations that fit their interests and values.

Non-cognitive KSAOs and general cognitive abilities are stable since they stem from how personality evolves over time and cannot be modified significantly by advances in education and/or experience (Kanfer, 1990). The extant literature considers these characteristics as predictors of job performance and firm performance (Carroll, 1993; Schmidt & Hunter, 1998). KSAOs become part of an organization when they are combined with those owned by other employees and, thus, become higher-level human resources at the team or unit level.

However, the dynamic that allows for the combination and integration of KSAOs is not yet completely unpacked. To fill this void, the process leading to valuable unit-level human resources consists of two interrelated components. The first is "the complexity of the unit's task environment, or the degree to which the unit's tasks require interdependence and coordination among members" (Ployhart & Moliterno, 2011, p. 135). The second is defined as "enabling states and consists of the unit's behavioural processes, cognitive mechanisms, and affective psychological states" (Ployhart & Moliterno, 2011, p. 135).

In detail, with respect to the first component, Ployhart and Moliterno (2011) identify four dimensions that characterize the complexity of the task. The first dimension, *temporal pacing*, refers to employees' need to interact to complete a given task. This implies that face-to-face interaction is needed because information sharing is not enough. The second dimension is the *dynamism* of the task environment affecting the processes of organizational resource creation (Eisenhardt & Martin, 2000; Teece, 2007). Then, *task complexity* is another dimension of the interaction dynamic that requires the need to communicate with other team members. Finally, they suggest a fourth dimension, *workflow structure*, defined as "pooled, sequential, reciprocal, and intensive" (Ployhart & Moliterno, 2011, p. 136), as a feature in the creation of higher-order resources. Considered all together, these characteristics affect the creation of unit-level resources originating from individual KSAOs.

The second component of the process leading to valuable unit-level, *emergence enabling states*, that is, behavioral, cognitive, and affective, support the development of human resources at unit level, since they facilitate interaction among team members. These features are highly context and firm contingent, since they could be particularly relevant in the performance of some tasks and within some firms, while they could be completely irrelevant in the performance of another task at another company, as highlighted by the literature on the contribution of human resources to organizational performance at a micro level (Coff & Kryscynski, 2011).

These considerations summon a further characteristic to better investigate the contribution of human resources to competitive advantage, defined by Wright et al. (2014) as "malleability." Although the above characteristics (both cognitive and non-cognitive abilities) can be, to some extent, resistant to change, depending on the degree of malleability individual characteristics can be nurtured and developed over time. This introduces a further dimension in the context of human capital resources practices, especially with respect to their relationship with managerial decisions and, in turn, competitive advantage. More precisely, several strategy scholars have emphasized the relevance of *firm-specific, higher-order resources* and their contribution to organizational performance (Barney & Wright, 1998; Hatch & Dyer, 2004). In particular, they conceive of these resources as competences and capacities that allow firms to achieve competitive advantage. However, they warn that these resources are characterized by causal ambiguity and, also, non-transferability between and among firms. Furthermore, in order to understand how human resources contribute to competitive advantage at the organizational level, we must consider KSAOs' heterogeneity (Ployhart et al., 2014), since this affects the way human capital resources are combined and, in turn, higher-order resources can be shaped.

In summary, given the different issues emphasized by the examined perspectives, a multidisciplinary framework is needed to analyze the dynamics that allow for the identification of how individual KSAOs are available for units' purposes, along with the processes of combination and interaction among people with heterogeneous competences (Ployhart et al., 2014).

The development of this framework should help overcome the lack of internal consistency that limits the development of a holistic framework, thus providing an important advance to this area of research. To this end, Ployhart et al. (2014) integrate several contributions by decomposing human resources into three elements:

• what human resources are, to define their structure;
• what human resources do, to define their function; and
• the level at which they can be observed.

To contribute to the definition of human resource structure, they distinguish among different constructs proposed by the extant literature, thus clarifying the different levels of analysis. In detail, they define as individual differences the bundle of capacity, both cognitive and non-cognitive, owned by people, such as ability, personality, motivation, attitudes, and physical characteristics (see also Ackerman and Heggestad, 1997; Guion, 2011). However, emotion, motivation, and satisfaction cannot be defined as KSAOs because they are influenced by environmental conditions – only those individual characteristics that are relatively stable over time are conceived of as KSAOs. In turn, only those KSAOs that are linked with economic outcome can be defined as *human capital* (Ployhart et al., 2014).

Finally, *human capital resources* is defined as a subset of human capital. The distinction between these two constructs (i.e., human capital and human capital resources) is central to the development of a holistic theoretical framework and is relevant for the internal consistency of its main construct. Indeed, many studies use these concepts interchangeably, while other scholars state that human capital can exist only at the individual level, and that it cannot be directly available for the purpose of the firm (Nyberg, Moliterno, Hale, & Lepak, 2014).

By assuming that human capital is just a directly available individual-level resource, and not also a firm-level resource, many theoretical contributions have been overlooked or neglected. In particular, the studies that emphasize the contribution of individual differences of CEOs, top management, and star employees to organizational performance have been almost ignored (Carpenter, Sanders, & Gregersen, 2001; Groysberg & Lee, 2009; Hess & Rothaermel, 2011; Rosen, 1981; Rothaermel & Hess, 2007; Sanders & Hambrick, 2007; Zucker and Darby, 1996).

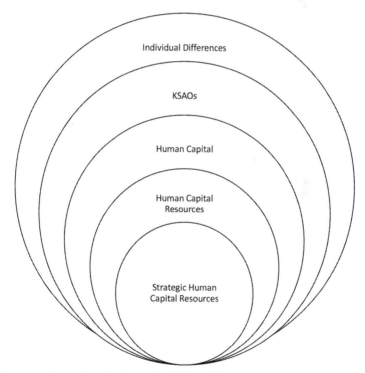

Individual Differences

KSAOs

Human Capital

Human Capital Resources

Strategic Human Capital Resources

Source:　Adapted from Ployhart et al. (2014), p. 375.

Figure 1.2　　*Human resources constructs*

In summary, human capital resources are those resources available for a unit's purpose (Ployhart et al., 2014) and among these resources a specific subset is strategically relevant in the quest for competitive advantage. In this case, human capital resources become *strategic human capital resources*. Figure 1.2 represents the distinction between these constructs, as introduced by Ployhart et al. (2014).

The literature examined so far and the model proposed by Ployhart et al. (2014) help us to depict a theoretical framework that improves construct validity of the phenomenon under observation. However, this investigation requires further exploration. In particular, the dynamic leading to the generation of human capital resources at the unit level needs a deeper analysis. More precisely, a tighter examination is required from the initial condition that allows for its generation (that is, the bundle of *individual differences*) to the final configuration of strategic human capital resources.

By adopting a resource microfoundation perspective, in particular, we can identify how individual capacity can become human capital for the organization, while from a macro perspective it is possible to identify the path to competitive advantage (Barney & Felin, 2013; Ployhart & Moliterno, 2011; Ployhart et al., 2014).

1.3   ADDRESSING NEW METHODOLOGICAL CHALLENGES

As noted above, one of the goals of this book is to address the methodological challenges that are hampering our understanding of the human capital resource at different levels. These challenges deal with some specific theoretical issues whose empirical investigation either did not provide us with convergent evidence or did not clarify adequately the dynamic under investigation. More precisely, among the challenges highlighted above are:

- a closer examination of the effect of human capital, observed through the theoretical lens of individuals' shared experience to clarify whether it is characterized by either a linear or a non-linear effect on organizational performance;
- the investigation of a potential agency conflict between firms' ownership/top management and the meso-managerial level constituted by middle managers, since the former are in charge of deciding whether

and when human capital should be renewed and the latter should proceed to new human capital integration at the team/unit level;

* an enquiry into the topics characterizing the debate in the human capital resource theoretical domain in order to identify the themes on which scholars from different perspectives are concentrating both conceptual developments and empirical efforts.

With respect to the first challenge, in the previous section we have observed that the dynamics that lead to the generation of higher-order resources (i.e., unit-level human resources) have remained underinvestigated (Ployhart et al., 2014). The extant literature maintains that a promising approach to exploring this topic is the research stream that focuses on shared experience among individuals belonging to the same team or organization. A large number of studies have investigated shared experience among team members as a phenomenon leading to the generation of higher-level resources, thanks to the combination of both cognitive and non-cognitive individual characteristics (see Berman, Down, & Hill, 2002 for a detailed examination of these studies). Shared experience stems from individual tacit knowledge combined with other team/unit members' individual tacit knowledge to generate new higher-order human resources at the team level. The interaction and the interdependence required to carry out a given task thus lead to the creation of team- or unit-level resources. If observed through this approach, higher-level human resources are no longer just an aggregation of heterogeneous individual characteristics, since they become a more complex phenomenon that links two of the elements suggested by Ployhart and Moliterno (2011), namely: (1) *the complexity of the unit's task* as a measure of the interdependence and coordination among members needed to complete the task; and (2) *enabling states*, which takes into account behaviors, cognitive mechanisms, and psychological states. These two elements affect the ability of the firm to generate human resources at team or unit level and, in turn, to make these resources viable sources of competitive advantage.

However, notwithstanding the distinguished contributions so far available, the extant research has not yet reached convergence with regard to the effects of higher-level resources on firm performance, especially concerning the dynamic of this effect (i.e., a linear vs a non-linear effect). In particular, some studies suggest a linear relationship between team members' shared experience and firm performance (Reagans, Argote, & Brooks, 2005), while other scholars maintain a non-monotonic relationship, which turns negative after a certain point due to knowledge ossification and predictability (Berman et al., 2002). In addition to the not yet achieved convergence on the effects of shared experience on organizational performance, the examination of these effects carries interesting implications for the renewal choices of human capital and, in particular, on the different actors/subjects interested by these choices that, for the sake of clarity in this volume, we identify with the firm's owner/top management and the middle manager in charge of deploying human capital at the unit/team level. If we assume a non-monotonic relationship (e.g., a non-linear effect that turns negative after a certain point) then the owner/top management must renew periodically and recurrently the bundle of human resources before the team/unit incurs negative results. On the other hand, if the relationship between shared experience and team performance is linear and positive, then renewal processes are infrequently needed and thus these must be carried out only in terms of a planned substitution of those individuals no longer available. Therefore, it is of the utmost importance to clarify whether the relationship between shared experience and performance is either linear or non-monotonic.

With regard to the second challenge, we suggest that it is appropriate to investigate the effect of both internal and external renewal factors (i.e., promotions, demotions, voluntary and involuntary turnover), and also how new human resources with different levels of cognitive and non-cognitive characteristics interact with other human resources already available and embedded at the firm level. This is quite a relevant issue, since the new competences and skills that a given owner decides to introduce within the unit/team is likely to affect an organization's short-term results, with an uncertain effect, perhaps negative. This occurrence, could, in turn, lead a middle manager (i.e., the meso-managerial level in our perspective) in charge of deploying the new human resources to implement a human capital strategy inconsistent with the owner's goal and desideratum.

To the best of our knowledge, to date, the extant research has not paid adequate attention to the *meso* level, but overlooking this occurrence hampers our understanding of employees' integration and development perception with regard to organizational tenure, job training, and organizational commitment. We maintain that overlooking the meso level constitutes critical neglect, since managers' performance is generally evaluated from a short-term time perspective, thus they could adopt opportunistic behavior if they deem that the top management/owner's human capital policy might negatively affect their unit performance.

In particular, a middle manager's decisions could negatively affect an owner's renewal policies and long-term strategies because the integration of new employees at the team level (owner's desideratum) may take time to yield the expected performance. As a result, middle managers might decide not to integrate these new resources in the context of a unit's processes to the extent required by the top management/owner. This, in turn, gives rise to an agency problem between the owner (or a given top manager) in charge of human resource renewal and the middle manager in charge of integration and development of human resources. We argue that addressing this issue may provide a quite interesting advance both with regard to macro-meso-managerial-level interactions and a deeper understanding of microfoundations in the context of managerial behavior at different levels of competence (Ployhart & Hendricks, 2019).

Finally, with regard to the third challenge highlighted above, we investigate the way scholars and researchers are approaching the evolution of the field, with respect, in particular, to its theoretical domain and the relevance of the most recurrent research topic. In particular, we analyze the main topics stemming from the debate on strategic human resources management, with the purpose of identifying a new approach focused on the development of a holistic framework capable of integrating both the micro- and the macro-level perspectives and to take account of the meso-managerial level in the context of human resources management. To this end, we used a data mining approach applied to the analysis of the articles published in the special issue of the *Journal of Management* (2014), "Strategic human capital: crossing the great divide" (Wright et al., 2014). The abstracts of these articles are reproduced in the appendix at the end of this chapter.

To carry out this analysis we employed a specific methodology, topic development, based on a novel data mining technique, KNIME Analytics, and its related word analysis technique, linear discriminant analysis. By means of these tools, we ran text mining analyses using the most well-known frequency measures of that analysis, that is, inverse document frequency (IDF) and term frequency (TF).

Thanks to this specific word processing methodology and text mining procedure, we constructed a flow chart to highlight the main issues of the debate and the potential ideas/concepts for "crossing the great divide" (Wright et al., 2014).

In Figure 1.3 we report the output of our elaboration using KNIME Analytics Platform 4.0.

Figure 1.3   Topic modeling on human capital

As shown in Figure 1.3, the word with the highest frequency is "Manager," which implies that this piece of literature seems to pay attention to a meso-managerial level. This is followed by the topics "Hire," "Market," and "Labor," which emphasizes the relevance of the methods adopted to acquire knowledge and skills. The presence of the topic "Compensation" testifies to the attention to HR practices in theoretical studies as well as in empirical efforts, since HR practices focus on the tools employed by managers to improve the contribution of employees to competitive advantage. On the contrary, the topics "Advantage," "Strategic," "Source," although aiming to emphasize the link between human resources and competitive advantage, seem to have received less attention from these contributions.

This invites our reflection on the micro level and the related link between individual characteristics and the performance of a specific task, and the potential relationship of these characteristics with a firm's endowment of knowledge and experience, and, in turn, with competitive advantage. In summary, from the content analysis carried out through this novel methodology, it seems that the following points deserve further reflection:

* A new research framework aiming at the reconciliation of the micro and macro levels deserves adequate effort and attention.
* The micro and the macro levels of analysis still appear quite separated in their research goals and theoretical foci.
* The meso level concerning the contribution of middle managers is quite overlooked.

1.4   CONCLUSION

The literature on human resources suggests that SHRM is a multifaceted construct made up of both cognitive and non-cognitive characteristics, whose features can be either generic or firm specific, both at the individual or unit level. However, its definition is a necessary, but insufficient condition with which to achieve an advanced and contemporary human resources management conceptual perspective since several research issues should be further investigated, such as:

* the dynamics leading to the creation of higher-order human resources (i.e., either at the team or the unit level);
* how to combine human resources within a given organization with respect to their endowment of both cognitive and non-cognitive abilities;
* how individuals' differences in the endowment of both cognitive and non-cognitive abilities interact;
* how to deal with the different levels of human capital (i.e., micro, meso and macro levels);
* how to manage a potential agency conflict between ownership and meso-managerial level of human resources.

In the following chapters, we take on the challenges highlighted in the previous sections and provide two focused empirical investigations and a novel conceptual framework to deal with the issues reported above. In particular, Chapter 2 endeavors to investigate whether the relationship between shared experience and performance is either linear or non-monotonic, while Chapter 3 examines how human capital renewal choices affect organizational performance and meso-level orientation towards cross-level cooperation with regard to human capital development. Finally, Chapter 4 provides a fresh conceptual framework for dealing with strategic human capital at the macro, meso, and micro levels.

NOTE

1.   Realistic, Investigative, Artistic, Social, Enterprising, and Conventional.

APPENDIX: PAPERS IN THE SPECIAL ISSUE OF THE *JOURNAL OF MANAGEMENT* (2014)

Wright, P. M., Coff, R., & Moliterno, T. P. (2014). Strategic human capital: Crossing the great divide [Editorial]. *Journal of Management*, *40*(2), 353–370.

Strategic human capital has emerged as an area of interest in both the strategy and human resources management literatures, yet these literatures have developed without adequate interdisciplinary conversation. The special issue on strategic human capital sought to bridge this divide through creating a platform for researchers from both fields to engage in dialogue. In addition to commenting on both the journey and destination of the special issue, we explore the manifestations of this divide and identify six issues that emerged that could provide areas of common interest across the two fields.

Ployhart, R. E., Nyberg, A. J., Reilly, G., & Maltarich, M. A. (2014). Human capital is dead; long live human capital resources! *Journal of Management*, *40*(2), 371–398.

This paper introduces a radically different conceptualization of human capital resources that runs counter to the individual-level approaches that have dominated human capital theory for the last 50 years. We leverage insights from economics, strategy, human resources, and psychology to develop an integrated and holistic framework that defines the structure, function, levels, and combinations of human capital resources. This multidisciplinary framework redefines human capital resources as individual or unit-level capacities based on individual knowledge, skills, abilities, and other characteristics (KSAOs) that are accessible for unit-relevant purposes. The framework and definition offer three broad contributions. First, multidisciplinary communication is facilitated by providing precise definitions and distinctions between individual differences, KSAOs, human capital, human capital resources, and strategic human capital resources. Second, given that human capital resources originate in individuals' KSAOs, multiple distinct types of human capital resources exist at individual and collective levels, and these types are much more diverse than the historical generic-specific distinction. Third, the multiple types of human capital resources may be combined within and across levels, via processes of emergence and complementarity. Consequently, the locus of competitive advantage has less to do with whether human capital resources are generic or specific but instead occurs because nearly all human capital resource combinations are complex, are firm-specific, and lack strategic (or efficient) factor markets. Overall, the proposed multidisciplinary framework opens new avenues for future research that challenge the prevailing literature's treatment of human capital resources.

Mackey, A., Molloy, J. C., & Morris, S. S. (2014). Scarce human capital in managerial labor markets. *Journal of Management*, *40*(2), 399–421.

Strategic human capital scholars are increasingly recognizing the importance of human capital scarcity for explaining individual and firm outcomes. This article focuses on scarce human capital in the top manager labor market – and in particular, patterns in which top managers and firms form employment relationships. This examination redirects strategic human capital scholarship in three important ways. First, the findings point to the importance of specifying an omission from prior human capital scholarship: the relationship between human capital and the firm's resource base (e.g., potential complementarities). Second, the article illustrates the need to simultaneously consider both human capital scarcity and complementarities and reinforces that scarce human capital can indeed be general human capital. Finally, the theory explains how complementarities fundamentally alter value creation and appropriation dynamics. Specifically, complementarities facilitate the matching of the best managers and firms with the most productive resources, increase the size of the pie (financial proceeds) from the employment relationship, and can enhance the manager's bargaining power in the division of these proceeds.

Liu, X., Van Jaarsveld, D. D., Batt, R., & Frost, A. C. (2014). The influence of capital structure on strategic human capital: Evidence from U.S. and Canadian firms. *Journal of Management*, *40*(2), 422–448.

Strategic human capital research has emphasized the importance of human capital as a resource for sustained competitive advantage, but firm investments in this intangible asset vary considerably. This article examines whether and how external pressures on firms from capital markets influence their human capital strategy. These pressures have increased over the past three decades due to banking deregulation, technological innovation, and the rise of institutional investors and new financial intermediaries. Against this backdrop, this study examines whether a firm's capital structure as measured by share turnover, shareholder concentration, and financial leverage is associated with firm investment in strategic human capital. Based on survey and objective financial data from 221 establishments in the United States and Canada, our analysis indicates that firms with greater share turnover, higher shareholder concentration, and higher levels of financial leverage are less likely to invest in human resource systems that create strategic human capital. Differences in national financial systems also lead to differential effects for U.S. and Canadian firms.

Tzabbar, D., & Kehoe, R. R. (2014). Can opportunity emerge from disarray? An examination of exploration and exploitation following star scientist turnover. *Journal of Management*, *40*(2), 449–482.

How do the specific characteristics of a departing star influence the effects of the star's turnover on a firm's innovation processes? Proposing a contingency model of key employee turnover, we argue and demonstrate that the individual characteristics of a star scientist who exits a firm determine the effects of the star's turnover for the organization. Based on a longitudinal study of star scientist turnover in the biotechnology industry (1972–2003), we show that while star turnover disrupts existing innovation routines and thus decreases exploitation, this "shock" creates opportunities for the firm to search beyond existing knowledge boundaries, thereby increasing exploration. However, these effects are moderated by the departing star's innovative and collaborative involvement within the firm. Specifically, the results indicate that a departing star's innovative involvement strengthens the negative effects and weakens the positive effects of the star's turnover on exploitation and exploration in the firm, respectively. On the other hand, a departing star's collaborative involvement within a firm strengthens the negative effect of the star's exit on exploitation but increases the positive effect of star turnover on exploration, thereby fostering opportunities for technological renewal. We suggest therefore that the prognosis for firms losing stars may vary, and may not always be dire. Our findings indicate that the short-term and long-term value of human capital is contingent on the social mechanisms surrounding its utilization. Thus, we offer a redirection for research and extend the resource-based view and human capital theory by introducing a resource dependence perspective into this theoretical context.

Brymer, R. A., Molloy, J. C., & Gilbert, B. A. (2014). Human capital pipelines: Competitive implications of repeated interorganizational hiring. *Journal of Management*, *40*(2), 483–508.

This article offers pipelines as a new perspective on human capital heterogeneity between firms. Using resource-based theory logic, we define pipelines as repeated interorganizational hiring and a practice firms use to differentially acquire and accumulate human capital and mitigate human capital risks. Pipelines are a ubiquitous staffing practice with ambiguous implications for firm performance that to date have eluded scholarly examination. Thus, we use a systems framework to highlight input, output, and process contingencies in which pipeline hiring can create advantage over rivals – contingencies of human capital scarcity in the labor market, the choice of firm activity system, and product market ambiguity (i.e., credence qualities), respectively. Collectively, the article's theoretical foundations provide new insights for human resource, strategy, and human capital fields and open the conceptual space of pipelines for examination by organizational scholars. We discuss the theoretical, empirical, and practical implications accordingly.

Crocker, A., & Eckardt, R. (2014). A multilevel investigation of individual- and unit-level human capital complementarities. *Journal of Management*, *40*(2), 509–530.

Human capital theory has recently expanded to include multilevel analysis by conceptualizing the unit-level human capital resource. At the same time, the value of complementary resources has been theorized to provide competitive advantages for firms. Thus, human capital at one level in the firm may impact the performance of human capital at another level in the firm if the resources are complementary. Through a multilevel analysis performed using hierarchical linear modeling of Major League Baseball data, we show that the relationship between individual human capital and individual performance is impacted by complementary functional and managerial unit-level human capital resources. As such, this paper contributes to the understanding of how complementary multilevel human capital resources relate to performance outcomes. Implications of our findings include support for the notion that more is not always better when it comes to high-quality human capital and that unit-level human capital plays an important role in performance of individual-level human capital.

Campbell, B. A., Saxton, B. M., & Banerjee, P. M. (2014). Resetting the shot clock: The effect of comobility on human capital. *Journal of Management*, *40*(2), 531–556.

In this paper, we examine how employee mobility impacts the human capital of both those who are new to the organization (movers) and those who are existing members (incumbents). Employee mobility events can disrupt both the location-specific and the colleague-specific components of human capital and thus have different impacts on overall human capital. We test our theory on the disparate effects of location change and personnel change on human capital in the highly interdependent context of the National Basketball Association. We find that movers experience adverse performance shocks after mobility events that are moderated when moving as a group, and we also find that group mobility events hinder the performance improvement of incumbents. Our findings are consistent with the limited transfer of location-specific human capital and the disruption of colleague-specific human capital after mobility events.

Khanna, P., Jones, C. D., & Boivie, S. (2014). Director human capital, information processing demands, and board effectiveness. *Journal of Management*, *40*(2), 557–585.

Research on human capital as a source of competitive advantage has focused largely on firm employees. In this article, we argue that outside directors' general human capital can also be a source of competitive advantage. Firm performance is likely to benefit from directors' human capital – that is, their prior experience and education – because such human capital is likely to make them more effective at monitoring management and providing advice. Drawing on insights from research on individuals' cognitive limitations, we further argue that the extent to which the firm is able to benefit from this human capital can be severely limited by the demands for information processing that directors face from their other board positions. Consequently, we find that the benefit of directors' human capital is contingent upon the information processing load placed upon them from their other board appointments. We find support for our hypotheses using data on over 5,700 directors from 650 firms sampled from the Fortune 1000. This study extends the nascent literature on board human capital by showing that in addition to specific expertise in relevant areas, directors' general human capital can also help firms create competitive advantage. The theory developed in this article also contributes to the literature on strategic human capital by incorporating the concept of information processing demands, suggesting that not only do such demands leave limited cognitive capacity for directors to focus on the focal firm but also that they can severely diminish the beneficial effects of directors' general human capital.

Grigoriou, K., & Rothaermel, F. T. (2014). Structural microfoundations of innovation: The role of relational stars. *Journal of Management, 40*(2), 586–615.

Conceptualizing new knowledge development as a process of search and recombination, we suggest that a focus on individual productivity alone presents an undersocialized view of human capital. Rather, we emphasize the importance of embedded relationships by individuals to effectively perform knowledge-generating activities. We rely on intraorganizational knowledge networks emerging through individual collaboration to identify actors who can positively influence their organization's knowledge outcomes. We study two types of such relational stars: integrators (outliers in centrality) and connectors (outliers in bridging behavior). We test our ideas using the patenting portfolios of 106 pharmaceutical firms from 1974 to 1998 predicting the effect of relational stars on their firm's quantity and quality of inventive output – proxies for the firm's capacity to develop more and better new knowledge stocks. We find that the presence of relational stars results in firm-level knowledge advantages not only through their own superior recombinant efforts, but also through their capacity to make others around them more effective at knowledge recombination. Relational stars are firm-specific, and their advantages are socially complex and causally ambiguous because they rely on a network of within-firm interactions. Relational stars, therefore, are prime candidates to be a source of sustainable firm-level knowledge advantage.

Liu, K. (2014). Human capital, social collaboration, and patent renewal within U.S. pharmaceutical firms. *Journal of Management, 40*(2), 616–636.

Human capital has received much attention as the microfoundation for a firm to achieve competitive advantage. For knowledge-intensive firms, inventors' human capital plays an important role in developing intellectual assets such as patents. Little research, however, has explored how inventors' human capital influences the firm's decisions of which patent to maintain or to abandon. This study investigates the effects of inventors' human capital and collaboration characteristics on patent renewal decisions in the context of U.S. pharmaceutical firms. The results show that having star inventors on the inventor team, having more coinventors, and having inventors from multiple locations significantly increase chances of patent renewal. In addition, having more coinventors positively moderates the effects of star inventors on patent renewal. Implications for research are discussed.

2. Understanding and clarifying the dynamics of strategic human capital effects on performance: A quasi-replication of major literature evidence

2.1 STRATEGIC HUMAN CAPITAL EFFECTS ON PERFORMANCE: ISSUES AND AMBIGUITY

In Chapter 1, we pointed out that the extant literature has paid attention to the relationship between individuals' characteristics and performance, meanwhile neglecting to investigate how tacit knowledge sharing affects performance, thus overlooking a quite important dimension in the context of strategic human resource management (SHRM). In this chapter, therefore, we endeavor to investigate how tacit knowledge and shared experience are conveyed into higher-order resources and how this process affects organizational performance.

According to Nonaka and Takeuchi (1995), tacit knowledge may be acquired through experience-based processes, such as socialization and internalization, while subsequent studies have recognized other mechanisms that lead to new tacit knowledge creation, such as shared experience (Berman, Down, & Hill, 2002; Reagans, Argote, & Brooks, 2005), and learning by doing (Swap, Leonard, Shields, & Abram, 2001). A peculiar trait of tacit knowledge is that it is difficult to transfer and imitate. This is a double-edged sword, since, on the one hand, it protects strategic human capital (SHC) from imitation; on the other hand, however, the very tacit nature of SHC also hampers its diffusion throughout the organization. This may lead to important limitations with regard to the most appropriate deployment of human capital resources at the organizational level, since it is difficult to transfer team-based tacit knowledge to other people, especially when these people are newly acquired human resources.

Several studies have examined the impact of individual tacit knowledge on the accumulation of new knowledge at both the team and the organizational levels (Berman et al., 2002; Castanias & Helfat, 1991; Coff, 1999; Dokko, Wilk, & Rothbard, 2009; Reagans et al., 2005). However, because people differ in the way they accumulate knowledge (Holcomb, Holmes, & Connelly, 2009), these differences influence team-based tacit knowledge, since accomplishing complex tasks requires the coordination of heterogeneous knowledge assets (Berman et al., 2002). This is particularly important for people who work in the same organization (or team) and need to transfer their tacit knowledge to co-workers. To emphasize the importance of this process, Weick and Roberts (1993) adopted the metaphor of the collective mind.

To address the inherent complexity concerning knowledge-creation and knowledge-sharing processes, the extant literature has examined not only the mechanisms that lead to the creation of new knowledge, but also those processes that allow for knowledge transfers within the organization. With regard to knowledge creation, prior studies have emphasized the role of path dependence, temporal compression, and firm-specific components (Kogut & Zander, 1992) as focal factors that lead to valuable knowledge creation. With regard to knowledge transfer, instead the literature has focused on human capital dimensions as drivers of knowledge transferability within and across different levels of human capital (Nyberg, Fulmer, Gerhart, & Carpenter, 2010). Thus, to better understand how individual skills can be combined at the collective level (for example, at the team level), it is important to examine the mechanism underlying both the creation and the transferability of collective tacit knowledge to other individuals (Berman et al., 2002; Reagans et al., 2005) and/or to other organizations (Castanias & Helfat, 1991; Holcomb et al., 2009).

Succinctly, the development of tacit knowledge at the collective level depends on the execution of complex tasks over time. Yet, as noted above, this is a mixed blessing, since, on the one hand, the inherent nature of tacit knowledge protects against rivals' imitation, and, on the other hand, this occurrence hampers its diffusion within the organization. This, in turn, hinders the creation of an organization's collective mind (à la Weick & Roberts, 1993), thus limiting the development of valuable SHC. The focal point is therefore to understand what dynamics allow for the creation of team-level tacit knowledge, and in turn, of SHC at the firm level.

Recent studies suggest that sharing complex tasks and practices represents dynamics that may advance tacit knowledge creation at the collective level (Reagans et al., 2005). But, although the extant research has demonstrated that experience sharing is a leading practice in the diffusion of tacit knowledge from an individual level to a team level, the link between shared experience and competitive advantage requires further exploration at both the conceptual and empirical levels. In particular, it should be further explored whether the link between shared experience and competitive advantage is linear, or, after a certain threshold, this effect is attenuated or even turns negative because of other intervening phenomena.

In particular, one of the theoretical points that may require further theoretical development is represented by the contribution of teams' tacit knowledge to organizational performance. Indeed, the collective endowment of tacit knowledge constitutes a stock of practices and competences available at a given time, and it is generally assumed (see Katz, 1982) that, after a certain period of time, this stock will no longer contribute to the firm's competitiveness, mostly due to inertia and ossification (Berman et al., 2002).

More precisely, inertia and ossification may occur because, while performing complex tasks and practices, teams' knowledge becomes routinized, thus engendering both positive and negative effects. The positive side of these effects is due to the reduction of the probability of errors, which is a critical success factor, for instance, in the context of airline crew and surgical operations (Reagans et al., 2005). However, knowledge routinization is also supposed to reduce the likelihood of discovering different ways to perform complex tasks, which is a negative occurrence, especially when firms face environmental changes. Under these circumstances, according to Levinthal and March (1993), core competences become traps and, thus, what used to be source of competitive advantage evolves, subsequently, into a core rigidity (Leonard-Barton, 1995).

With this premise in mind, the focus of this chapter is to investigate the effect of teams' shared experience on firms' results. Previous research has demonstrated that teams' shared experience fosters coordination among team members (Berman et al., 2002), thanks to specific features such as the development of rules and procedures shared at the team level; the awareness that a team's members will follow such rules; and the increased communication among team members. However, at the same time, shared experience may become a source of inertia and rigidity, especially when firms face environmental change. Therefore, the overall net effect of shared experience on performance is ambiguous. However, there is another important and almost neglected issue in the context of knowledge-sharing and knowledge-creation processes at the team level that requires further examination, namely, the effect of role and task specificity. More precisely, we maintain that shared experience at team level is likely to exert a different effect on organizational performance, depending on whether a given team's task/role is either mainly routinized or mostly creative. Routinized tasks could benefit from shared experience because repeated collective practices become more efficient and require less time to be carried out, as testified by the learning curve approach (Reagans et al., 2005). Creative tasks, instead, are more oriented towards exploring and introducing change and thus the presence of a collective routine could hinder this orientation. However, this point requires further reflection because creative roles too can benefit from shared experience. In particular, in cases of a sudden and unplanned change, when an unforeseen decision must be taken, the presence of collective routines increases the chances that the team members will better understand what must be done.

In essence, collective routines and shared experience (i.e., collective mind à la Weick & Roberts, 1993), improve the ability to adjust to and align with unpredicted changes, an occurrence that is likely to support innovation without losing efficiency. Unfortunately, we have no detailed studies or empirical research devoted to the investigation of the impact exerted by different roles (in terms of either creative or routinized role content) on teams' performance, which hampers a better and fine-grained understanding of how collective knowledge may contribute to competitive advantage.

In summary, the impact of teams' shared experience has been a central argument in the debate regarding SHRM; however, the effect exerted by shared experience in the context of different organizational roles/tasks has been largely neglected. To fill this void, our study contributes to the literature by extending Berman et al.'s (2002) analysis. More precisely, our contribution is twofold. First, we develop a quasi-replication analysis by using the same main variables in a different population (Bettis, Helfat, & Shaver, 2016). Second, we introduce a novel measure concerning the study's main variable with respect to the appraisal of shared experience by adopting Reagans et al.'s (2005) measure.

2.2   LESS, AFTER A CERTAIN POINT, IS MORE: INVESTIGATING THE PRESENCE OF MONOTONIC AND NON-MONOTONIC RELATIONSHIPS

Previous studies have highlighted how individual tacit knowledge can contribute to the creation of team tacit knowledge (Kogut & Zander, 1992; Weick & Roberts, 1993). However, what may require further theoretical development and empirical investigation is the relationship between collective tacit knowledge and performance, in order to better understand how collective tacit knowledge contributes to organizational success and competitive advantage. This is important, since, on the one hand, it seems to offer a positive contribution to organizational results, given the improvement in coordination among team members and their lower number of mistakes; on the other hand, however, tacit collective learning also gives rise to rigidity, which in turn makes firms less reactive to market change.

Furthermore, prior studies on shared experience have emphasized firms' ability to create a distributed base of shared knowledge and how this may lead to competitive advantage (Berman et al., 2002; Reagans et al., 2005). However, the empirical evidence reports a more nuanced pattern with regard to its effects on performance, mostly because of the presence of knowledge ossification in the context of this relationship. In detail, Berman et al. (2002) provided support for their hypothesis regarding a negative impact of shared experience on performance, after a certain point. However, when examining the actual observed data, they found no observations concerning shared experience levels on the decreasing side of the slope. Differently stated, Berman et al.'s (2002) hypothesis regarding a quadratic relationship between shared experience and performance was supported from an algebraic and econometric standpoint; however, no observation empirically supported the actual negative effect after a certain point. Therefore, we can conclude that Berman et al.'s (2002) actual result is not an inverted-U-shaped relationship; rather, they observed a relationship that reported an increasing effect, which increases with a decreasing rate, since the downward side of the U-shape is empty of observations. However, other studies that investigated the relationship between shared experience and performance reported different results. For example, Reagans et al. (2005) reported a linear and positive relationship between team experience and organizational performance. More precisely, they provided support to the relationship between team shared experience and the time required to complete a surgical procedure by observing that the greater the operating team shared experience, the lower the time required to perform the operation, and the better the results.

In summary, it seems that there is no convergence among extant studies with respect to the effect that shared knowledge exerts on performance. For this reason, we suggest a re-examination of Berman et al.'s (2002) study by proposing its quasi-replication in order to provide robustness and generalizability to their findings (Bettis et al., 2016).

2.3   A QUASI-REPLICATION OF MAJOR, YET AMBIGUOUS, EMPIRICAL EVIDENCE

2.3.1   Berman et al. (2002) Results Summary

Berman et al. (2002) provide one of the main contributions to the investigation of the relationship between shared experience at the team level and performance. The authors theorize a non-monotonic relationship characterized, first, by an increasing trend at decreasing rates, since sharing tacit knowledge from an individual level to a collective level leads to an improvement in coordination and therefore in team performance, and, subsequently, to a reduction of this effect due to an ossification phenomenon associated with an increasing difficulty to change. More specifically, they develop several hypotheses, which we summarize in Table 2.A1.

The authors test their hypotheses in the context of the National Basketball Association (NBA). The total number of teams examined is 23 and represents the entire population of the team participating in this league from the 1980–81 season through the 1993–94 season.

Berman et al. (2002) adopt two *dependent variables*: (1) the *number of wins for each season* for each team; and (2) the number of *total regular assists*[1] for each team during a season (for a more detailed analysis of these measures, see Berman et al., 2002).

The main *independent variable* the authors employed to test their hypotheses was *shared team experience*. They define shared experience as the collective tacit knowledge that originates from training and deploying the members of a team. To assess shared experience, the authors sum the number of years a player has played in the team as a proxy for the experience gained in the team, weighted for the minutes of actual play during the season. Since the number of current players in the team forms the basis of the shared tacit knowledge during that specific season, they obtain an average value of the shared tacit knowledge between the team members. In particular, they maintain that: "shared team experience . . . is a proxy for the value of the stock of tacit knowledge held in the collective mind of a team" (Berman et al., 2002, p. 21). Moreover, to test the existence of a non-monotonic relationship, they create another measure, *team experience squared*, that is, the squared value of shared team experience, which is a measure that allows for the appraisal of a non-monotonic relationship between shared team experience and team performance.

As in any research, to account for other factors affecting the dependent variables, they introduce several control variables:

- *average draft[2] position*, a measure that assesses the quality of the players; the higher the draft position, the higher the supposed quality of a basketball player;
- *average age*, the average age of players, crucial in this setting since the ability of players tends to deteriorate quickly;
- *coaching experience*, measured as the number of years spent as a coach in a specific team;
- *standard deviations of age* and *standard deviations of draft position* to assess, respectively, the heterogeneity in the average age of the player and in the draft position.

For a detailed explanation of these measures see Berman et al. (2002).

The authors used a pooled time series model to test the study's main hypotheses and we can observe that they find general support for their hypotheses. Table 2.A2 reports their main results.

The results reported in Table 2.A2 provide support for hypotheses H1a and H1b. More precisely, they observed a positive and significant effect of shared experience on both the dependent variables analyzed with regard to hypothesis H1a; then they observed a negative and significant value of shared experience squared, with respect to hypothesis H1b. In addition, to corroborate the negative relationship between shared experience and firm performance after a certain point, they compute partial derivatives of their models with respect to shared experience. This allows them to obtain the precise amount of shared experience beyond which its effect on performance becomes negative. However, this further investigation reported that no observed values were found in the actual research data that were employed to test Model 1, while just a few actual observations were found with regard to Model 2. This led the authors to conclude that, given the results obtained, the negative relationship between shared experience and firm performance after a certain point should be maintained only from a theoretical standpoint, while the actual data supported the existence of a positive effect, at a decreasing rate, between shared experience and performance.

To clarify this issue, we suggest that a re-examination of Berman et al.'s (2002; henceforth, BDH) main research goal could provide an important contribution with regard to the relationship between shared experience and team performance. To achieve this, we proceed through the following steps:

1. First, we propose a quasi-replication of BDH, maintaining the same research design, including measures, method, and model but employing a different population (Bettis et al., 2016).
2. Second, to investigate the existence of a more fine-grained, within-team effect in the context of the shared experience phenomenon, we take account of the tasks associated with the different roles in a team. We decided to apply this distinction in order to understand whether there are differences in the effect that shared experience exerts on performance. In particular, we examine a team's role depending on whether this role is characterized by a mainly creative or a mostly routinized content. To pursue this task, we introduce a different measure with regard to both team shared experience and organizational performance.
3. Finally, to corroborate both the empirical and the theoretical relevance of our study, we propose a quasi-replication by employing a different measure of team shared experience. In particular, we adopt the measure developed by Reagans et al. (2005; henceforth, RAB). By means of this measure, in their study the authors observed a positive linear relationship between the shared experience and the reduction of time required to perform a specific surgical operation.

In summary, in our model we test the effect of shared experience on performance by employing both BDH and RAB measures, also taking account of creative and routinized roles and adopting a different research setting, the Italian "Serie A" professional football league.

2.3.2   Re-examining the Role of Shared Experience in the Context of the Italian Serie A Football League

In order to provide additional evidence to prior studies, to clarify ambiguous phenomena, and/or to further explore non-converging results, replication studies can take different forms. According to Bettis et al. (2016), replication studies may vary depending on the source of the data and the research design. Through those two dimensions, they identify the different types of replication, or quasi-replication, that can be carried out. Table 2.A3 shows the different types of quasi-replication and their purposes.

Following the clarifying information reported in Table 2.A3, the aim of our replication is twofold. First, we aim to extend previous evidence to other environmental settings by using a different population to test the same hypotheses; second, we aim at increasing research robustness by using a different measure of prior research's main variable, namely, team shared experience. More precisely, our goal is to analyze the effect of shared experience on team performance to ascertain whether it is either linearly positive, or increasing at a decreasing rate, or non-monotonic (i.e., U-shaped or inverted-U shaped).

Accordingly, our quasi-replication is focused on hypotheses H1a and H1b of Berman et al.'s (2002) study, which state (Berman et al., 2002, p. 19):

H1a: There is a positive relationship between shared team experience and team performance. This relationship is subject to diminishing returns. The positive performance effect of shared experience will decline as shared experience grows.

H1b: After some point in time, the relationship between shared team experience and team performance will become negative as the costs of knowledge ossification start to outweigh the benefits of cumulative experience.

2.3.2.1   Method
Setting
Our research setting is the Italian Serie A professional football league. Similar to other business settings, the Italian Serie A represents a highly competitive context, wherein players must perform complex tasks whose

execution relies on tacit knowledge. In this context, team members must coordinate in order to achieve a positive result for their team (that is, to win a given game). Team members' coordination involves role heterogeneity, since football players are highly specialized athletes who fulfill specific roles, such as goalkeeper, defender, midfielder, forward. For the purpose of this study, we decided to cluster these roles into two main categories, namely, offensive players and defensive players. In particular, defensive players include the goalkeeper and the defenders, while offensive players include midfielders and forwards. According to the empirical research on the strategic orientation of teams, offensive players are oriented to adopt creative solutions and tactics, whereas defensive players are inclined to follow routinized procedures (for a detailed examination of offensive and defensive attitudes in the context of human capital, see Woolley, 2011). This approach allows us to understand whether shared experience affects in a differentiated fashion those complex tasks at the team level, since we maintain that these tasks are characterized by a different degree of creativity.

In particular, we surmise that shared experience at the team level contributes to the improvement of teams' practices, mainly because of the improvement of team coordination and its routine consolidation. However, these improvements represent a double-edged sword, since some practices could evolve into areas of resistance to change and inertia, which in turn hinders changes in existing practices. In particular, when changes take place at the industry level, the existence of established routines implies the inability to adapt quickly to a changed competitive environment.

Data
Our dataset includes the entire population of teams participating to the Italian Serie A professional football league from the 1960–61 to the 1991–92 seasons. Although we exploit our data at year level, we collected data on a game-day basis, since we construct our measures on the basis of single game-day observations. Furthermore, we collected our data at the individual player level in order to assess the phenomena of interest of our study, and to investigate the implication of this information in the context of football teams. Our main sources of data are *Enciclopedia Panini del Calcio Italiano, 1960–2000* (2000) and *Almanacco Illustrato del Calcio* (years 1960–91), which are among the most authoritative and accurate sources of information on Italian football, especially concerning richness of information in the time span covered by our research.

With regard to the time window of our research, we found some changes in the population of football teams participating in the Serie A league. In particular, from the 1960–61 through the 1966–67 seasons and from the 1988–89 through the 1991–92 seasons, 18 teams played in Serie A, whereas from the 1967–68 through the 1987–88 seasons there were only 16 teams. Given these contingencies, our dataset contains 32 football seasons (years), with 16 802 game-day observations. This occurrence gives rise to an unbalanced panel; in addition, it should be considered that at the end of each season the teams that occupy the lowest positions in the final ranking (usually the last three teams) are relegated to the lower league, Serie B; at the same time, Serie B's best teams (usually, the first three teams), are upgraded to Serie A.

Dependent variables

Because the purpose of this study is to replicate extant researches on shared experience, we employ three different dependent variables. Each variable deals with a specific performance measure already adopted by previous studies. In addition, since we advance an extension and quasi-replication of BDH, we also introduce new measures with regard to the effect of human capital shared experience. More precisely, we use the following measures of performance:

- *Team performance.* This is calculated as the mean points obtained by a given team at the end of the season (total number of points obtained in a season divided by the total number of games in that season). For each game, a team obtains two points for a win, one point if the match is draw, and none for a loss. In football, to win a match it is necessary to score more goals than those conceded to the opponents.
- *Team offensive performance.* This measures the number of goals scored by a team for each game. We assume that this variable is the most appropriate measure of performance to appraise the contribution of creative human capital, which in our study is represented by offensive players. Similar to other studies carried out in the context of sports settings, the ability to score goals is considered a compelling measure of organizational performance, especially with respect to offensive performance (Berman et al., 2002; Holcomb et al., 2009; Sirmon, Hitt, Ireland, & Gilbert, 2011). Both the professional (Foot, 2007; Sconcerti, 2009) and academic (Palacios-Huerta, 2016; Szymanski, 2015) literature agree that scoring goals is predictive of a successful performance, as a team that is unable to score goals

will obviously not be able to win any matches. The rationale of this assumption is that a team that is unable to score goals suggests that its offensive schemes are predictable and not sufficiently creative.

Finally, since we also aim to investigate the contribution of different team roles, we introduce another specific measure of performance:

- *Team defensive performance.* This measures the number of goals conceded to the opponent team during a given game. The lower the number of conceded goals, the better a team's defensive performance.

Independent variable
Team shared experience (calculated following BDH) is the independent variable. Since the aim of our study is to carry out a quasi-replication, we use the measure introduced by BDH, which is calculated as follows: the total number of games played by a team's players in a season multiplied by the number of years that a given player has played for that team. The product of these two terms is then divided by the number of players in the team's roster in that season. The analytic measure is:

$$\sum_{i=1}^{n} \frac{(Number\ of\ games\ played\ by\ a\ player \times player's\ tenure\ with\ a\ given\ team)}{Number\ of\ players\ in\ the\ team's\ roster}$$

where:
I = all of a team's players included in the roster, from 1 to n;
n = total number of players in a team's roster;
number of games played by a player is the number of games played by each player at the end of a season;
player's tenure with a given team is the number of years that a player has played with a given team, including the current one;
number of players in the team's roster is the total number of players included in a team's roster.

Furthermore, since the aim of our research is also to provide a better understanding of the contribution of different roles in the context of knowledge-sharing processes, we introduce two different measures of shared experience to take account of specific roles at the team level:

- *Shared experience of offensive players* is measured as the number of games that offensive players have played together during the season, multiplied by the number of years these players has played for that team, and divided by the number of players in the team's roster.

- *Shared experience of defensive players*, likewise, is measured as the number of games that defensive players have played together during the season, multiplied by the number of years these players has played for that team, and divided by the number of players in the team's roster.
- *Shared experience of offensive players squared* is obtained as the square of *shared experience of offensive players*. We calculate this measure to test the non-monotonic effect of shared experience of these players on performance.
- *Shared experience of defensive players squared*, likewise, is obtained as the square of *shared experience of defensive players*. We calculate this measure to test the non-monotonic effect of shared experience of these players on performance.

Control variables
To provide our analyses with accuracy and robustness we must account for the several contingencies that could affect a team's performance. Accordingly, the control variables used in our models aim to consider the variability of our dependent variables at different levels. In particular, we introduce control variables at the organizational level, team level, and the middle management level:

- *Organizational level:*
  - *Historic aspiration level.* This variable measures the historical relevance of a given team in the context of the Serie A league. It is obtained by weighing the average of the ranking positions achieved by a specific team in all the previous seasons. In particular, we assign a weight equal to 25 percent for the ranking position achieved at the end of the previous season, and a weight equal to 75 percent for the average value of all of the previous years. Finally, we multiply this value by −1 in order to make the regression results more intuitive and interpretable, since the best performances with respect to this measure are associated with the lowest values, and the worst teams are associated with the highest values. For instance, for any given ranking, the value 1 is the lowest and, at the same time, the best position in that specific ranking.
- *Team level:*

- *Team quality* appraises the quality of the players following a two-step procedure, first at the individual level and then at the team level. First, we calculate the number of games played by a given player with his team during each season, and then we multiply this figure by the team's total points at the end of that season; finally, we divide this number by the age of the player. The motivation for this measure is as follows. Since Italian football is an extremely selective and competitive environment, it is difficult for a Serie A player to be continually in the starting line-up (Brera, 1975; Sconcerti, 2009). Therefore, a player who plays a large number of games per season is a high-quality professional player, from an athletic, technical, and disciplinary point of view. This value is calculated for each year, up to the previous season with respect to the player considered. This measure is used to assess the quality of each player; subsequently, the average value of the whole team is calculated. We validated this measure by employing other proxies of players' quality and achieved a remarkable convergence.
- *Standard deviation of team quality* is the standard deviation of team quality and is calculated in order to assess heterogeneity with regard to the quality of players in the context of a specific football team.
- *Team's mean age* is the average age of all the team's players. This is a quite relevant control variable with respect to the quality of any player, with few exceptions. More precisely, a player's age represents a sort of double-edged sword because, on the one hand, it is understood as a proxy of experience; however, on the other hand, it is related, after a certain point, to the declining value of a player's quality.
- *Standard deviation of team age* is the standard deviation of the team's age and it is calculated to assess age heterogeneity of the players included in a specific football team's roster.
- *Middle management level:*
  - *Coach's tenure* gauges the specific experience that a coach has acquired as a manager of a professional football team, and it is measured as the number of seasons he spent with that team.
  - *Coach's absolute tenure* appraises a manager's experience at the whole Serie A level as a coach, and it is measured as the number of seasons a coach spent in the Serie A league.

• Finally, we control also for the time effect, which is measured through a "year-effect" dummy variable.

Model specification

Following the model specification adopted by Berman et al. (2002), we employed a time series cross-sectional panel dataset. We set a "team-day-year" unit of observation, and a "team/year" unit of analysis. More precisely, we collect data at individual (player) level; in addition, we use the game-day as the study time variable. This approach allows us to compute measures both at the team and the organizational levels, and to organize our dataset at team-year level.

Furthermore, we conducted a Durbin-Wu-Hausman test (instead of using a pooled time series), which reported significant results, and then we specified a fixed-effects panel regression that controlled for omitted variables that were time-invariant and therefore were absorbed by fixed effect. We used Stata 15 SE (command: xtreg, fe) and we also specified robust estimation to control for autocorrelation (Bergh, 1995), also accounting for standard errors at team level by means of a clustering procedure that accounts for firm-specific residuals between teams (Bowen & Wiersema, 1999; Greene, 2003).

2.3.2.2 Results

Descriptive statistics and the bivariate correlation matrix are reported in Table 2.A5. To account for multicollinearity, we calculated the variance inflation factor (VIF) coefficient to estimate the extent to which the variance of a coefficient is inflated because of linear dependence with other predictors. Our analysis reported VIF values below 10, commonly accepted as the threshold of serious multicollinearity. Moreover, some variables included in our models are linear combinations of other variables (that is, squared values of these variables or the standard deviation of them). However, this is not a bias for our study, since the *p*-value for those variables is not affected by multicollinearity.

Table 2.A4 reports the results of our quasi-replication analysis of BDH. Our regression models examine the linear and the quadratic effects, respectively, of shared experience on team performance. In particular, Model 1 is the baseline model reporting control variables. Model 2 reports the results of the study's main variable. In particular, the coefficient of team shared experience is positive and significant ($\beta = 0.00256$ and $p < 0.01$), thus providing support for a linear relationship between team shared experience and performance. Finally, Model 3 examines the existence of a non-monotonic relationship between team shared experience and performance in order to investigate the ossification process of knowledge and its decreasing performance. However, we did not find support for the ossification process of knowledge, since the coefficient of team shared experience squared is positive but not significant. Therefore, our quasi-replication analysis does not support the non-monotonic, quadratic relationship theorized by Berman et al. (2002).

Because our replication's results do not support BDH findings, we offer an extension of this study in order to investigate whether shared experience could, nonetheless, exert a non-monotonic effect on team performance, depending on whether a team's members carry out either creative or routinized tasks.

To pursue this goal, we analyzed the effect of team shared experience of defensive players and offensive players separately, assuming, respectively, the former as a routinized role and the latter as a creative one. We decided to assume defensive roles in the context of the Italian Serie A, and of modern football in general, as routinized roles, since all the defensive players of a football team must execute coordinated moves whose practice is carried out several times per day during weekly training sessions under the supervision of a team's coach. In particular, defenders must be respectful of the distance between and among them, of the simultaneous move they must make under the specific contingencies of a game, and of the characteristics of the opponents. Therefore, although it could be assumed that defenders play their role on a mostly individual basis, the action of defending in the context of a professional football team is, instead, mostly a coordinated collection of routinized moves.

Moving beyond the domain of professional football, it should be noticed that routinized tasks, in particular, benefit from increasing coordination among co-workers, since it reduces the amount of time required to carry out a given task and the likelihood of making mistakes, thanks to the collective stance (à la Weick & Roberts, 1993) that is generated when individual tacit knowledge becomes collective knowledge shared among team members. When applied to the domain of football, the effect of routinized knowledge deserves further investigation, since, on the one hand, a team must defend its goal on a collective basis and not as a sum of skilled individuals, and thus coordination among all of the defenders is a fundamental piece of collective knowledge; on the other hand, it has been argued that tacit knowledge at a collective level is doomed by ossification, inertia, and competency traps; thus, it is important to introduce at a given point in time some changes to prevent these mostly negative contingencies.

Therefore, we investigate the existence of a non-monotonic relationship in the context of defensive football roles, because, according to BDH, shared knowledge, first, generates a positive effect due to an increase in coordination between team members; however, this effect is diluted, over time, for the above reasons, thus determining a decreasing performance after a certain point.

Table 2.A6 reports the descriptive statistics and bivariate correlation matrix. There is no evidence of multicollinearity affecting the results, since the observed values of variance inflation factors are below 10 (Chatterjee, Hadi, & Price, 2000). Table 2.A7 reports the results of shared experience of defensive players on team defensive performance (a measure that assessed the number of goals scored by the rival team). In particular, Model 1 deals with the relationship between shared experience of defensive players and the number of goals conceded to the opponent team in a football game, that is, the extent to which defenders' shared experience prevents the opposing team from scoring goals. However, we did not find support for this hypothesis. More precisely, we found that the shared experience of defensive players reduces the likelihood that the opposing team will score, but this finding is non-significant. In addition, we also investigate the existence of a non-monotonic relationship between shared experience of defensive players and performance. Model 2, however, reports a non-significant coefficient of shared experience of defensive players squared. Therefore, insofar as role specificity in the context of defensive players is concerned, we did not find support for the non-monotonic relationship between shared experience among defensive players (which we assumed as routinized roles) and team performance.

Finally, we test the effect of shared experience in the context of offensive players, a role we defined as creative. Table 2.A8 provides descriptive statistics (means, standard deviations, and correlations), while Table 2.A9 reports the OLS regression results. First, it can be observed that there is no evidence of multicollinearity affecting our results, as we ran variance inflation factors (VIF command with Stata 15 SE, after the running regression model with time effect) and all our models reported VIF values below 10 (Chatterjee et al., 2000).

Model 1 reports the study control variables and explores the existence of a linear relationship between shared experience of offensive players and performance (which is assessed as the number of scored goals at the end of the season, a straightforward assessment of the extent to which these specific roles – that we assumed as creative – were able to contribute to teams' performance). Model 2 deals with shared experience of offensive players squared, a measure we introduced to assess the existence of a non-monotonic relationship between shared experience of offensive players and performance. We found a positive, statistically significant coefficient for shared experience of offensive players, which supports the hypothesis of linear relationship on team offensive performance ($\beta = 0.163$, $p < 0.01$). Instead, the coefficient of shared experience of offensive players squared was not significant and thus this empirical evidence rules out the non-monotonic effect of shared experience on performance and corroborates the linear relationship above reported.

To provide further robustness to our results, we also ran other analyses, employing different dependent variables. More precisely, we adopted a different measure of team performance, calculated as the mean point gained by a given team at the end of the season. These new analyses confirmed the results already obtained through the analyses reported above.

2.4   AN EXTENSION: INTRODUCING A NEW VARIABLE TO ASSESS A TEAM'S SHARED EXPERIENCE

2.4.1   Method

According to BDH, shared experience is a complex phenomenon to observe and measure. Indeed, they argue that:

> [E]xperience playing together can obviously be measured in several ways with a variety of variables. We are not attempting, however, to argue that the method we have chosen is the only acceptable measure, but, rather, that it is a reasonable measure of experience and provides a straightforward means of investigating the relationship between tacit knowledge and performance. (Berman et al., 2002, p. 21)

Thus, to increase the robustness of our analysis, we decided to adopt a different measure to assess team experience, which is introduced and developed by Reagans et al. (2005) (RAB). In particular, RAB analyze how to leverage the knowledge accumulated by others in order to improve team performance in the context of healthcare (i.e., a distinguished teaching hospital). Starting from the analysis of learning curves – according to which it is possible to observe how production costs decrease as experience increases – the authors analyze how different types of experience can determine a different contribution to performance. They investigate people's experience at three different levels: individual, organizational, and team. In detail, they define each of them as follows:

> Individual experience – the cumulative production history of any one individual – provides an individual with an opportunity to become more proficient at his or her tasks and at performing established routines and practices. Organizational experience – the cumulative production history of the organization – provides the organization with the opportunity to identify more productive routines and practices. As the organization gains more experience, each individual has more opportunities to benefit from knowledge accumulated by others. Experience working together – the cumulative production history of pairs of individuals – provides individuals with the opportunity to learn who knows what, resulting in a more efficient division of labor. And, with increased experience working together, individuals become more willing to share knowledge and information, increasing their ability to coordinate across their specialized roles. We examine the contribution of each kind of experience to performance. By considering how much each kind of experience affects performance. (Reagans et al., 2005, p. 870)

Then, to assess the shared experience, first they introduce a measure for individual experience and subsequently a measure for team experience, as follows (Reagans et al., 2005, p. 873; original emphasis):

> *Individual experience*. For each person involved in a procedure, we calculate the number of times that he or she has performed the procedure, not including the current procedure. This variable is *IKi*. We sum across these individual values and divide by team size to define the level of individual knowledge on the team, $\sum_{i=1}^{N} Ni = 1$ *IKi/N*, where *N* is number of people on the team. The variable indicates the amount of individual knowledge available to the team. Our prediction for organizational experience relates team performance to the knowledge accumulated by people outside the focal surgical team. Our organizational experience includes the cumulative experience of people on the focal team. To test our prediction for organizational experience, we subtract the cumulative experience of individuals inside the focal team from cumulative organizational experience. While we expect both individual and organizational experience to be important, past research generally distinguishes between the two. In addition, the evidence indicates that while both kinds of experience improve performance, focal units benefit from their own experience more than they benefit from knowledge accumulated outside their unit (Argote et al. 1990, Baum and Ingram 1998).
> *Team experience*. For each pair of individuals on a team, we calculate the number of times that the pair has performed the procedure with each other in the past, not including the current procedure. This variable is *RKij*. We sum

across pairs on the team and divide by the possible number of pairs to define the level of relationship-specific knowledge available to the team:

$$\sum_{i=1}^{N}\sum_{j=1}^{N} RKij/N(N-1)/2.$$

where N is team size and $RKij$ is the number of times that person i has operated with person j. The variable indicates the average amount of experience that team members have working with each other. Although we call our indicator of individual knowledge "individual experience," it is important to be clear about what the variable is not. Individual experience is not the number of times that each team member has performed a procedure by himself. A total joint replacement is an interdependent task, and knowledge is accumulated while working with other people. In a perfect design, we would have knowledge accumulated while working alone and knowledge accumulated while working with others. We could then examine the association between each kind of knowledge and performance. However, given how knowledge is accumulated, our analytical strategy is to estimate the effect that individual (the number of times the individual performed the procedure) experience has on team performance. That individual experience could have been accumulated while working with people on the current team or with people outside the team. The team experience effect, therefore, indicates the additional effect that experience working together has on team performance.

Therefore, following RAB's procedure, we calculate three different types of shared knowledge. The first considers the knowledge shared by all of a team's members, while the other two consider the knowledge shared, respectively, only by defensive and offensive players, considered separately, as a team's subunits.

Our goal is twofold: first, we aim to analyze whether there is a non-monotonic relationship between team shared experience and performance; second, we aim to investigate whether shared tacit knowledge has a different effect on team performance in the context of creative or routinized tasks when these are analyzed separately.

2.4.1.1 Model specification

As reported above, since our aim is to extend BDH's analysis, we adopt a different measure of team shared experience. To carry out our analyses, we employ panel dataset with player-day-year as a unit of observation and team-year as a unit of analysis. In particular, we use the first level (player-day-year) to assess measures at individual and day-match level, while the latter (team-year) to test our hypotheses. Also for the following models we specified a fixed-effects panel regression that controlled for omitted time-invariant variables absorbed by fixed effect. We used Stata 15 SE (command: xtreg, fe), and we also specified robust estimation to control for autocorrelation (Bergh, 1995) with a clusterization for the standard error at team level. This accounted for firm-specific residuals between teams (Bowen and Wiersema, 1999; Greene, 2003).

2.4.2   Results

In this section, we report the test of the focal hypotheses developed by BDH. In particular, we present a different measure of team shared experience introduced by RAB to assess the non-monotonic relationship between the experience shared among the members of an organizations and performance.

By following the RAB procedure we calculate three different types of team shared knowledge. The first considers the knowledge shared by all team members, while the other two consider only the knowledge shared by defenders and attackers, respectively. In particular, our aim is to analyze whether team shared experience exerts a different effect depending on the nature of a given organizational role (i.e., either creative or routinized).

First, we analyze the general team shared experience with no distinction regarding the specific role of players. Model 1 in Table 2.A10 reports the descriptive statistics and correlations. To investigate the presence of multicollinearity, we ran the VIF procedure to estimate the extent to which the variance of a coefficient is inflated because of linear dependence with other explaining variables. Our analysis reports VIF values below 10, thus suggesting that multicollinearity is not a concern. Moreover, it should be noticed that some variables in our models are constructed as a linear combination of others (i.e., squared or standard deviation of a measure already employed in our models). However, the *p*-value of these variables is not affected by the multicollinearity.

Table 2.A11 reports our results for the regression analysis. More precisely, Model 1 presents the results for our control variables only. Model 2 reports the effect of team shared experience. As reported, the effect of shared experience is positively associated with team performance (β = 0.0164, *p*-value < 0.001). This result provides support to the hypothesized positive and linear relationship between the shared knowledge and the team performance. Model 3 reports the non-monotonic relationship hypothesized by BDH. To test this hypothesis, we introduce the squared value of shared experience; however, the coefficient for this variable was not significant. In sum, these results seem to confirm the existence of a linear relationship between shared experience and team performance, while we did not find support for a non-monotonic, quadratic relationship.

Next, we analyze the effect exerted by shared experience at the team level, with respect to specific tasks and organizational roles (i.e., defensive and offensive roles, respectively). Table 2.A12 reports our results for these analyses. In particular, Model 1 reports the means, standard deviations, and correlations for defensive players, whom we assumed were players involved in routinized roles. Similarly to our previous analyses, in this case, too, we ran the VIF analysis, following the same procedure we ran above, and likewise our results reported VIF values below 10, which allows us to not concern about multicollinearity (Chatterjee et al., 2000).

Table 2.A13 reports OLS regression results. Model 1 reports our test of a linear relationship between the shared experience of defensive players and performance, while Model 2 reports the coefficient of the hypothesized non-monotonic relationship. More precisely, Model 1 reports a negative and statistically significant coefficient for shared experience of defensive players (RAB) ($\beta = -0.673$, $p < 0.01$), thus providing support for the hypothesis dealing with the linear relationship between shared experience in the context of this specific role and performance. In particular, in this case our dependent variable is the number of goals scored by rival teams, thus, the lower this value the better the performance. However, Model 2 shows a positive and significant coefficient of shared experience of defensive players squared (RAB) ($\beta = 0.0808$, $p < 0.05$).

Thus, in the case of routinized tasks, shared experience, observed through collective tacit knowledge, seems to negatively affect a team's effectiveness after a certain point. To ascertain the precise value of the function after which this negative effect actually intervenes, that is, the actual point of the function after which its corresponding value turns from positive into negative, we follow BDH procedure. Specifically, first, we take the partial derivatives of Model 2 with respect to shared experience of defensive players (dp); then, we set its result equal to zero; and finally we calculate the level of shared experience at which we observed the beginning of a negative effect. More precisely:

Model 2:

δ *Defensive player performance/δ Shared experience of defensive players*
= −2.296 + 0.0808 × *shared experience of dp* = 0.
Shared experience of dp = 28.41

The value of 28.41 of shared experience of defensive players is not encompassed in our dataset. Thus, the support for this hypothesis is weak and can be accepted only from a theoretical viewpoint.

This implies that, when tacit knowledge is shared in the context of a team wherein routinized tasks are carried out, the effectiveness with which these routinized tasks are performed increases at a decreasing rate, up until a certain point, which represents the maximum of the observed function. This maximum represents the limit, which is constituted, in turn, by the actual limitations of the type of knowledge that it is possible to deploy in the context of a team-level, routinized procedure or task.

Finally, we report the results of our analyses in the context of creative roles. Table 2.A14 reports means, standard deviations, and correlations. We ran the required analyses to rule out potential multicollinearity concerns; in particular, VIF values were below 10, thus providing evidence that multicollinearity is not a concern (Chatterjee et al., 2000).

Table 2.A15 reports the results concerning shared experience of offensive players (*op*) whom we assumed were individuals carrying out creative roles. In particular, Model 1 estimates the linear effect of shared experience of offensive players on the likelihood to score goals. Consistently with the hypothesis of a linear relationship, a team's shared experience in the context of creative task was positively related to performance and statistically significant (β = 0.596; $p < 0.001$). Model 2 reports the results for shared experience of offensive player squared, our main explanatory variable of interest. The negative and statistically significant coefficient for this variable supports the non-monotonic relationship between shared experience and performance (β = −0.0312; $p < 0.1$). This curvilinear relationship is consistent with the study's main hypothesis, which maintained that as the shared experience of offensive players increases, performance increases too, yet at a decreasing rate. This implies that the effect of shared experience in the context of creative roles has a positive effect on the performance of a given organization up to a certain threshold, beyond which the effect is either diluted or can even turn negative. To further explore this result, we follow BDH; more precisely, first we took the partial derivatives of Model 2 with respect to the shared experience of offensive players, then we set the result equal to zero, and finally we calculated the level of shared experience at which negative returns started to set in. More precisely:

Model 2:
δ *Offensive player performance/δ Shared experience of offensive players*
= 1.450 – 0.0312 × *shared experience of op* = 0.
Shared experience of op = 23.2

Values higher than 23.2 were found only for a few observations in the context of our dataset, thus the support for a non-monotonic relationship between the shared experience of offensive players and performance is weak. However, it can be surmised that an ossification process could intervene in the context of creative roles, especially when collectively shared tacit knowledge is not frequently refreshed and renewed.

2.5 MANAGING STRATEGIC HUMAN CAPITAL IN TEAMS: A DISCUSSION OF OUR MAIN RESULTS

In this chapter we have examined the role of team members' shared experience on organizational performance with the purpose of providing a quasi-replication and an extension of BDH, who reported a non-monotonic relationship between team members' shared experience and organizational performance. More precisely, they empirically observed that the effect of a team's shared experience on performance increases at a diminishing rate, but after a certain point this rate could become negative because, first, the amount of knowledge available in a specific time period can be considered as fixed and, second, because a process of ossification can take place, which makes it difficult for a team to adapt to environmental changes. However, even if their findings theoretically support their assumption concerning the existence of a non-monotonic relationship, they did not find actual empirical observations in their dataset beyond the point after which negative returns on performance actually set in (and only a few observations for one of the two models reported in their study).

To further investigate the main issue of this, unfortunately, non-conclusive study, we employed a different population and a different assessment of the main issue of interest, and then replicated the hypothesized non-monotonic relationship between a team's shared experience and organizational performance. More precisely, we proposed two different approaches to conduct a quasi-replication of BDH. First, we used the same research design and the same measure with regard to a team's shared experience, adopting a different population for our empirical investigation and collecting our research data for a much longer period (32 years, between 1960 and 1992).

Table 2.A16 summarizes our main results through the comparison of the findings of the original study carried out by BDH with our quasi-replications, and with our extension carried out following RAB's measure. More precisely, Table 2.A16 reports our findings, subdivided into three levels of observation – team, defensive players and offensive players. At the team level, we observed a positive linear relationship between shared experience and performance, while we did not find support for a quadratic, non-monotonic relationship between team shared experience and organizational results.

Subsequently, we divided our research sample into two subsamples, defensive players and offensive players, whom we assumed had routinized and creative roles, respectively. Then, we ran our replication of BDH by employing their measure of shared experience on these two subsamples. We did not find support for a linear relationship in the context of routinized roles (defensive players), while we found instead a positive and linear relationship for creative tasks (offensive players). With regard to the investigation of a quadratic, non-monotonic relationship, we neither found empirical support for defensive players nor for offensive players. Therefore, our quasi-replication and extension of BDH, conducted through their original measure of shared experience, supported only the existence of a linear, positive relationship at the overall team level and in the context of creative roles (offensive players), while our data did not support the existence of a non-monotonic relationship in the form of an inverted-U shaped relationship, or in terms of an increasing effect at a decreasing rate.

Furthermore, in our quasi-replication study, we introduced an extension. More precisely, in order to increase the robustness of our analysis, we replicated the analysis proposed by BDH using an alternative measure of shared experience – that introduced and developed by RAB. The results of the analyses obtained through this different measure confirm the linear relationship between team shared experience and performance. In particular, we found a positive and linear relationship for all three levels of our investigation – team, defensive players, and offensive players. However, when we ran our test of the non-linear relationship between shared experience and performance, we did not find support for it at the team level, whereas we observed the existence of a non-monotonic relationship in the context of both routinized and creative roles. More precisely, both routinized and creative tasks reported an increasing effect on performance, at a decreasing rate. Yet, in the context of defensive roles, we had no observations in our dataset beyond the function's turning point, which implies that shared experience in the context of routinized tasks probably has no actual negative effect on performance, but only an increasing effect observed with a decreasing rate.

With regard to the creative roles (i.e., the task of offensive players in our study), our data reported just a few observations after the function's turning point. Thus, albeit in a very few cases, shared experience in the context of creative tasks may have a negative effect after a certain point because shared collective knowledge may be affected by inertia and rigidity, which indeed may negatively affect the execution of a creative task.

NOTES

1. An assist is attributed to a player who passes the ball to a teammate in a way that leads to a score by a field goal, meaning they were "assisting" in the basket.
2. A draft is the process used to allocate certain players to teams. In a draft, teams take turns selecting from a pool of eligible players.

APPENDIX

Table 2.A1   Berman et al. (2002): Hypotheses summary

H1a	There is a positive relationship between shared team experience and team performance. This relationship is subject to diminishing returns. The positive performance effect of shared experience will decline as shared experience grows
H1b	After some point in time, the relationship between shared team experience and team performance will become negative as the costs of knowledge ossification start to outweigh the benefits of cumulative experience
H2	Coaching experience with the same team interacts non-monotonically with shared team experience to affect performance. The positive performance effects of coaching experience with the same team will decline as shared experience grows
H3	Tenure heterogeneity will be negatively associated with organizational performance

Source: Berman et al. (2002).

Table 2.A2   Berman et al. (2002): Results summary

Variables	Model 1 Wins	Model 2 Assist
Constant	6.96 (15.00)	1671.80*** (353.10)
Shared experience	0.0063*** (0.0014)	0.17*** (0.03)
Shared experience squared	−2.6E-7** (1.03E-7)	−9.9E-6*** (2.6E-5)
Average age	0.53 (0.57)	0.47 (13.39)
Coaching experience	1.45* (0.61)	15.14 (13.84)
Player quality	−4.13** (1.57)	66.45† (38.29)
Experience coaching	0.0002† (0.000096)	−0.0006 (0.0022)
Experience heterogeneity	0.0004 (0.0005)	−0.0138 (0.0005)
Player quality heterogeneity	3.03 (2.03)	−25.73 (48.50)
Age heterogeneity	0.01 (0.78)	−5.77 (19.14)
−2 log likelihood	919.71	918.24

Note: $n = 322$. Unstandardized regression coefficients are shown, with standard errors in parentheses. † $p < 0.10$; * $p < 0.05$; ** $p < 0.01$; *** $p < 0.001$.
Source: Berman et al. (2002).

Table 2.A3   *Types of quasi-replication analysis*

	Same Research Design	Different Research Design
Same data and sample	Checking for errors and/or falsification of results	Robustness to different measures, methods, and models
Same population with different sample	Reliability of data	Robustness to different measures, methods, and models
Different population (different context)	Generalize to new population	Generalize to new population and assess robustness

Source: Bettis et al. (2016).

Table 2.A4   *Results of quasi-replication of Berman et al. (2002)*

	Model 1	Model 2	Model 3
	Team performance	Team performance	Team performance
Mean team's age	0.0417**	0.0364*	0.0364*
	(0.0129)	(0.0140)	(0.0140)
Standard team age	−0.0481**	−0.0418**	−0.0416**
	(0.0152)	(0.0145)	(0.0146)
Team quality	0.0000171	−0.0000142	−0.0000140
	(0.0000309)	(0.0000304)	(0.0000303)
Standard team quality	−0.000477	−0.000543	−0.000540
	(0.000484)	(0.000522)	(0.000523)
Historic aspiration level	0.0116**	0.0100**	0.0100**
	(0.00363)	(0.00335)	(0.00341)
Coach's absolute experience	−0.00308	−0.00343	−0.00348
	(0.00301)	(0.00315)	(0.00313)
Coach's team experience	0.0127*	0.0107	0.0109
	(0.00604)	(0.00693)	(0.00717)
Shared team experience (BDH)		0.00256**	0.00294
		(0.000936)	(0.00192)
Shared team experience squared (BDH)			−0.00000273
			(0.0000120)
_cons	0.268	0.289	0.278
	(0.333)	(0.352)	(0.373)
R^2	0.173	0.197	0.197
N	420	420	420

Note: Standard errors in parentheses. $\dagger\, p < 0.10$, $*\, p < 0.05$, $**\, p < 0.01$, $***\, p < 0.001$. Year effects are available on request.

Table 2.A5   *Means, standard deviations, and correlations*

	Mean	S.D.	Min	Max	1	2	3	4	5	6	7	8	9
(1) Team performance	1	0.26	0.4	1.71									
(2) Shared team experience (BDH)	49.78	24.49	10.03	129.06	0.576 (0)								
(3) Shared team experience squared (BDH)	3076.59	2899.63	100.69	16655.34	0.549 (0)	0.967 (0)							
(4) Mean team's age	25.2	1.13	21.75	28.38	0.155 (0)	0.219 (0)	0.241 (0)						
(5) Coach's team experience	1.96	1.54	1	10	0.299 (0)	0.381 (0)	0.366 (0)	0.071 (-0.099)					
(6) Team quality	1687.17	1025.92	0	4482.72	0.506 (0)	0.831 (0)	0.791 (0)	0.301 (0)	0.33 (0)				
(7) Standard team quality	91.3	50.4	0	239.48	0.384 (0)	0.706 (0)	0.682 (0)	0.197 (0)	0.265 (0)	0.894 (0)			
(8) Standard team age	4.18	0.9	1.81	11.65	-0.049 (-0.261)	0.141 (-0.001)	0.137 (-0.001)	0.012 (-0.791)	0.061 (-0.159)	0.255 (0)	0.339 (0)		
(9) Historic aspiration level	-7.45	3.63	-15.25	-1	0.648 (0)	0.602 (0)	0.571 (0)	0.146 (-0.003)	0.304 (0)	0.617 (0)	0.496 (0)	-0.007 (-0.88)	
(10) Coach's absolute experience	4.64	4.08	1	21	0.172 (0)	0.342 (0)	0.289 (0)	-0.001 (-0.986)	0.434 (0)	0.346 (0)	0.359 (0)	0.148 (-0.001)	0.149 (-0.002)

Table 2.A6   Means, standard deviations, and correlations

	Mean	S.D.	Min	Max	1	2	3	4	5	6	7	8	9
(1) Team defensive performance	33.62	9.6	11	68									
(2) Shared experience of defensive players (BDH)	23.67	13.25	3.66	69.7	−0.47								
					0								
(3) Shared experience of defensive players squared (BDH)	735.35	798.17	13.36	4858.09	−0.42	0.96							
					0	0							
(4) Mean team's age	25.2	1.13	21.75	28.38	−0.076	0.191	0.215						
					−0.078	0	0						
(5) Coach's team experience	1.96	1.54	1	10	−0.235	0.375	0.366	0.071					
					0	0	0	−0.099					
(6) Team quality	1687.17	1025.92	0	4482.72	−0.517	0.763	0.699	0.301	0.33				
					0	0	0	0	0				
(7) Standard team quality	91.3	50.4	0	239.48	−0.49	0.679	0.632	0.197	0.265	0.894			
					0	0	0	0	0	0			
(8) Standard team age	4.18	0.9	1.81	11.65	−0.07	0.162	0.144	0.012	0.061	0.255	0.339		
					−0.106	0	−0.001	−0.791	−0.159	0	0		
(9) Historic aspiration level	−7.45	3.63	−15.25	−1	−0.454	0.51	0.486	0.146	0.304	0.617	0.496	−0.007	
					0	0	0	−0.003	0	0	0	−0.88	
(10) Coach's absolute experience	4.64	4.08	1	21	−0.219	0.354	0.315	−0.001	0.434	0.346	0.359	0.148	0.149
					0	0	0	−0.986	0	0	0	−0.001	−0.002

Table 2.A7   *Shared experience by task: The effect of shared experience of defensive players (based on Berman et al.'s 2002 measure)*

	Model 1	Model 2
	Team defensive performance	Team defensive performance
Mean team's age	−0.883*	−0.865*
	(0.429)	(0.418)
Standard team age	1.412**	1.416**
	(0.454)	(0.455)
Coach's team experience	0.304	−0.276
	(0.272)	(0.290)
Team quality	−0.000437	−0.000473
	(0.00121)	(0.00119)
Standard team quality	0.0108	0.0119
	(0.0243)	(0.0241)
Historic aspiration level	−0.000389	−0.00999
	(0.200)	(0.204)
Coach's absolute experience	0.152	0.149
	(0.0918)	(0.0924)
Shared experience of defensive players	−0.0135	0.0898
(BDH)	(0.0506)	(0.126)
Shared experience of defensive players		−0.00156
squared (BDH)		(0.00162)
_cons	51.63***	49.70***
	(10.42)	(10.24)
R^2	0.255	0.256
N	420	420

Note: Standard errors in parentheses. † $p < 0.10$, * $p < 0.05$, ** $p < 0.01$, *** $p < 0.001$. Year effects are available on request.

Table 2.A8   *Means, standard deviations, and correlations*

	Mean	S.D.	Min	Max	1	2	3	4	5	6	7	8	9
(1) Team offensive performance	33.62	11.56	11	83									
(2) Shared experience of offensive players (BDH)	25.8	13.6	5.73	72.83	0.342 (0)								
(3) Shared experience of offensive players squared (BDH)	850.56	886.16	32.84	5304.69	0.325 (0)	0.969 (0)							
(4) Mean team's age	25.2	1.13	21.75	28.38	0.104 (−0.016)	0.211 (0)	0.217 (0)						
(5) Coach's team experience	1.96	1.54	1	10	0.222 (0)	0.322 (0)	0.294 (0)	0.071 (−0.099)					
(6) Team quality	1687.17	1025.92	0	4482.72	0.272 (0)	0.755 (0)	0.711 (0)	0.301 (0)	0.33 (0)				
(7) Standard team quality	91.3	50.4	0	239.48	0.121 (−0.005)	0.615 (0)	0.583 (0)	0.197 (0)	0.265 (0)	0.894 (0)			
(8) Standard team age	4.18	0.9	1.81	11.65	−0.121 (−0.005)	0.103 (−0.017)	0.099 (−0.022)	0.012 (−0.791)	0.061 (−0.159)	0.255 (0)	0.339 (0)		
(9) Historic aspiration level	−7.45	3.63	−15.25	−1	0.58 (0)	0.551 (0)	0.514 (0)	0.146 (−0.003)	0.304 (0)	0.617 (0)	0.496 (0)	−0.007 (−0.88)	
(10) Coach's absolute experience	4.64	4.08	1	21	0.04 (−0.356)	0.27 (0)	0.216 (0)	−0.001 (−0.986)	0.434 (0)	0.346 (0)	0.359 (0)	0.148 (−0.001)	0.149 (−0.002)

Table 2.A9   Shared experience by task: The effect of shared experience of offensive role (on Berman et al.'s 2002 measure)

	Model 1	Model 2
	Team offensive performance	Team offensive performance
Mean team's age	1.506*	1.509*
	(0.662)	(0.666)
Standard team age	−0.852	−0.869
	(0.604)	(0.615)
Coach's team experience	0.562	0.557
	(0.377)	(0.377)
Team quality	−0.00149	−0.00154
	(0.00117)	(0.00118)
Standard team quality	−0.0242	−0.0238
	(0.0233)	(0.0236)
Historic aspiration level	0.763***	0.768***
	(0.0927)	(0.0935)
Coach's absolute experience	−0.168	−0.163
	(0.136)	(0.138)
Shared experience of offensive players (BDH)	0.163**	0.100
	(0.0504)	(0.150)
Shared experience of offensive players squared (BDH)		0.000867
		(0.00199)
_cons	10.60	11.58
	(16.05)	(15.90)
R^2	0.403	0.403
N	420	420

Note: Standard errors in parentheses. † $p < 0.10$, * $p < 0.05$, ** $p < 0.01$, *** $p < 0.001$. Year effects are available on request.

Table 2.A10   Means, standard deviations, and correlations

	Mean	S.D.	Min	Max	1	2	3	4	5	6	7	8	9
(1) Team performance	1	0.26	0.4	1.71									
(2) Shared team experience (RAB)	22.31	5.34	6.28	41.22	0.36 / 0								
(3) Shared team experience squared (RAB)	526.16	249.08	39.47	1698.81	0.344 / 0	0.984 / 0							
(4) Mean team's age	25.2	1.13	21.75	28.38	0.155 / 0	0.289 / 0	0.278 / 0						
(5) Coach's team experience	1.96	1.54	1	10	0.299 / 0	0.112 / −0.01	0.12 / −0.005	0.071 / −0.099					
(6) Team quality	1687.17	1025.92	0	4482.72	0.506 / 0	0.144 / −0.001	0.138 / −0.001	0.301 / 0	0.33 / 0				
(7) Standard team quality	91.3	50.4	0	239.48	0.384 / 0	0.182 / 0	0.168 / 0	0.197 / 0	0.265 / 0	0.894 / 0			
(8) Standard team age	4.18	0.9	1.81	11.65	−0.049 / −0.261	−0.186 / 0	−0.193 / 0	0.012 / −0.791	0.061 / −0.159	0.255 / 0	0.339 / 0		
(9) Historic aspiration level	−7.45	3.63	−15.25	−1	0.648 / 0	0.24 / 0	0.231 / 0	0.146 / −0.003	0.304 / 0	0.617 / 0	0.496 / 0	−0.007 / −0.88	
(10) Coach's absolute experience	4.64	4.08	1	21	0.172 / 0	0.152 / 0	0.144 / 0	−0.001 / −0.986	0.434 / 0	0.346 / 0	0.359 / 0	0.148 / −0.001	0.149 / −0.002

Table 2.A11   *Effect of shared experience on organizational performance (Reagans et al.'s 2005 measure)*

	Model 1	Model 2	Model 3
	Team performance	Team performance	Team performance
Mean team's age	0.0417**	0.00360	0.00327
	(0.0129)	(0.0144)	(0.0146)
Coach's team experience	0.0127*	0.0153*	0.0156**
	(0.00604)	(0.00598)	(0.00575)
Team quality	0.0000171	0.0000702*	0.0000723*
	(0.0000309)	(0.0000307)	(0.0000313)
Standard team quality	−0.000477	−0.00122**	−0.00127**
	(0.000484)	(0.000442)	(0.000451)
Standard team age	−0.0481**	−0.0119	−0.0114
	(0.0152)	(0.0132)	(0.0130)
Historic aspiration level	0.0116**	0.00876*	0.00874*
	(0.00363)	(0.00361)	(0.00354)
Coach's absolute experience	−0.00308	−0.00392	−0.00389
	(0.00301)	(0.00333)	(0.00331)
Shared team experience (RAB)		0.0164***	0.0246*
		(0.00308)	(0.00912)
Shared team experience squared (RAB)			−0.000176
			(0.000156)
_cons	0.268	0.625*	0.544†
	(0.333)	(0.302)	(0.279)
R^2	0.173	0.272	0.273
N	420	420	420

Note: Standard errors in parentheses. † $p < 0.10$, * $p < 0.05$, ** $p < 0.01$, *** $p < 0.001$. Year effects are available on request.

Table 2.A12   Means, standard deviations, and correlations

	Mean	S.D.	Min	Max	1	2	3	4	5	6	7	8	9
(1) Defensive player performance	33.62	9.6	11	68									
(2) Shared experience of defensive players (RAB)	9.52	2.69	2.73	19.02	-0.302 0								
(3) Shared experience of defensive players squared (RAB)	97.94	54.93	7.47	361.63	-0.272 0	0.981 0							
(4) Mean team's age	25.2	1.13	21.75	28.38	-0.076 -0.078	0.235 0	0.222 0						
(5) Coach's team experience	1.96	1.54	1	10	-0.235 0	0.113 -0.009	0.105 -0.015	0.071 -0.099					
(6) Team quality	1687.17	1025.92	0	4482.72	-0.517 0	0.189 0	0.17 0	0.301 0	0.33 0				
(7) Standard team quality	91.3	50.4	0	239.48	-0.49 0	0.245 0	0.217 0	0.197 0	0.265 0	0.894 0			
(8) Standard team age	4.18	0.9	1.81	11.65	-0.07 -0.106	-0.119 -0.006	-0.131 -0.002	0.012 -0.791	0.061 -0.159	0.255 0	0.339 0		
(9) Historic aspiration level	-7.45	3.63	-15.25	-1	-0.454 0	0.197 0	0.19 0	0.146 -0.003	0.304 0	0.617 0	0.496 0	-0.007 -0.88	
(10) Coach's absolute experience	4.64	4.08	1	21	-0.219 0	0.197 0	0.187 0	-0.001 -0.986	0.434 0	0.346 0	0.359 0	0.148 -0.001	0.149 -0.002

Table 2.A13   Shared experience by task: The effect of shared experience of defensive role (measure from Reagans et al., 2005)

	Model 1	Model 2
	Defensive player performance	Defensive player performance
Mean team's age	−0.230	−0.213
	(0.437)	(0.456)
Coach's team experience	−0.399	−0.370
	(0.263)	(0.258)
Team quality	−0.00134	−0.00144
	(0.00139)	(0.00140)
Standard team quality	0.0245	0.0277
	(0.0259)	(0.0251)
Standard team age	0.839†	0.781†
	(0.429)	(0.433)
Historic aspiration level	0.00772	0.0283
	(0.213)	(0.201)

	Model 1	Model 2
	Defensive player performance	Defensive player performance
Coach's absolute experience	0.191*	0.175†
	(0.0916)	(0.0911)
Shared experience of defensive players (RAB)	−0.673**	−2.296***
	(0.196)	(0.627)
Shared experience of defensive players squared (RAB)		0.0808*
		(0.0302)
_cons	44.42***	51.74***
	(9.625)	(9.664)
R^2	0.283	0.294
N	420	420

Note: Standard errors in parentheses. † $p < 0.10$, * $p < 0.05$, ** $p < 0.01$, *** $p < 0.001$. Year effects are available on request.

Table 2.A14   *Means, standard deviations, and correlations*

	Mean	S.D.	Min	Max	1	2	3	4	5	6	7	8	9
(1) Offensive player performance	33.62	11.56	11	83									
(2) Shared experience of offensive players (RAB)	12.59	3.23	3.44	25.3	0.215								
					0								
(3) Shared experience of offensive players squared (RAB)	168.99	86.51	11.82	640.33	0.208	0.982							
					0	0							
(4) Mean team's age	25.2	1.13	21.75	28.38	0.104	0.28	0.266						
					-0.016	0	0						
(5) Coach's team experience	1.96	1.54	1	10	0.222	0.092	0.107	0.071					
					0	-0.033	-0.013	-0.099					
(6) Team quality	1687.17	1025.92	0	4482.72	0.272	0.099	0.097	0.301	0.33				
					0	-0.022	-0.025	0	0				
(7) Standard team quality	91.3	50.4	0	239.48	0.121	0.12	0.112	0.197	0.265	0.894			
					-0.005	-0.006	-0.01	0	0	0			
(8) Standard team age	4.18	0.9	1.81	11.65	-0.121	-0.185	-0.184	0.012	0.061	0.255	0.339		
					-0.005	0	0	-0.791	-0.159	0	0		
(9) Historic aspiration level	-7.45	3.63	-15.25	-1	0.58	0.251	0.237	0.146	0.304	0.617	0.496	-0.007	
					0	0	0	-0.003	0	0	0	-0.88	
(10) Coach's absolute experience	4.64	4.08	1	21	0.04	0.094	0.088	-0.001	0.434	0.346	0.359	0.148	0.149
					-0.356	-0.03	-0.041	-0.986	0	0	0	-0.001	-0.002

Table 2.A15   Shared experience by task: The effect of shared experience of offensive roles

	Model 1	Model 2
	Offensive player performance	Offensive player performance
Mean team's age	0.78	0.723
	(−0.695)	(−0.704)
Coach's team experience	0.630†	0.660†
	(−0.372)	(−0.368)
Team quality	0.00106	0.00119
	(−0.00134)	(−0.00134)
Standard team quality	−0.0384	−0.0417†
	(−0.0239)	(−0.024)
Standard team age	−0.372	−0.302
	(−0.62)	(−0.607)
Historic aspiration level	0.803***	0.814***
	(−0.107)	(−0.102)
Coach's absolute experience	−0.165	−0.167
	(0.146)	(0.146)
Shared experience of offensive players	0.596***	1.450*
	(−0.148)	(−0.57)
Shared experience of offensive players squared (BDH)		−0.0312†
		(−0.0178)
_cons	19.62	15.55
	−15.6	−14.22
R^2	0.408	0.41
N	420	420

Note: Standard errors in parentheses. † $p < 0.10$, * $p < 0.05$, ** $p < 0.01$, *** $p < 0.001$. Year effects are available on request.

Table 2.A16   Summary of main results of quasi-replication of Berman et al. (2002)

Relationship Hypothesized	Team Shared Experience BDH (2002)			Team Shared Experience RAB (2005)		
	Team	Defensive	Offensive	Team	Defensive	Offensive
Linear	Positive and statistically significant	Not significant	Positive and statistically significant	Positive and statistically significant	Negative (on conceded goal, thus, in essence, positive in terms of observed effect and statistically significant	Positive and statistically significant
Non-monotonic	Not significant	Not significant	Not significant	Not significant	U-shaped (on conceded goal, thus, in essence inverted-U, in terms of observed effect)	Inverted-U shape

3. The effect of strategic human capital renewal on organizational results: An empirical examination in the Italian Serie A professional football league

3.1 ADDRESSING STRATEGIC HUMAN CAPITAL RENEWAL

In Chapter 2, we highlighted how shared tacit knowledge contributes to the development of higher-level resources and, in turn, to organizational performance. However, under specific circumstances, a given organization could, or should, release a portion of these higher-level resources.

Several factors may affect the release of higher-level resources. First, firms can experience either internal or external causes that lead to the release of some co-specialized resources; second, employee turnover, both voluntary and involuntary, and employee movement, such as promotions, transfers, and demotions, are associated with a release of co-specialized knowledge resources; third, macroeconomic conditions and industry trends also represent factors that can instigate a change in the composition of strategic human capital and, in turn, in a team's human capital configuration (Coff, 1997, 1999; Lepak & Gowan, 2010; Lepak & Snell, 1999). Finally, as reported in the previous chapter, we have empirically observed that shared experience positively affects team performance, albeit at a decreasing rate, an occurrence that could suggest the renewal of knowledge resources periodically to refresh a firm's strategic human capital.

Although strategic human capital renewal has been recurrently examined in the last four decades, some specific issues have not received adequate empirical investigation, nor has their theoretical underpinning been scrutinized with respect to several issues of interest, such as, for instance, organizational roles, industry, firm age and size, and so on. In addition, the extant literature reveals a void with regard to the effects of the release of co-specialized resources on team performance, which, in turn, implies there is no fine-grained understanding of how to proceed towards an effective renewal of strategic human capital (SHC). Therefore, in this chapter, we endeavor to investigate whether SHC renewal decisions affect performance, and how.

From a human capital management perspective, the purpose of SHC renewal is to regenerate current human capital endowment at the firm level and to introduce new expertise within a given unit/team. After the acquisition of new SHC at the firm level, the domain/industry expertise of newcomers must be integrated with current employees' expertise, which represents a team-level and collectively co-specialized type of knowledge (henceforth, current SHC co-specialization). In addition, SHC renewal involves a variety of managerial decisions that are usually adopted at different managerial levels. Because individuals in charge of SHC decisions at different levels may have level-specific goals and may assume conflicting stances, this occurrence invites, through an agency theory theoretical lens, a principal–agent (P–A) dispute.

Agency theory (AT) studies describe the separation of an organization's ownership from management, and advance that the objectives of the owner (principal) and those of the manager (agent) may not be aligned (Berle & Means, 1932; Eisenhardt, 1989; Fama & Jensen, 1983; Jensen & Meckling, 1976). From this perspective, P–A alignment is considered quintessential to effective and efficient management, and a number of AT studies warn of managerial mischief when there is misalignment (Dalton, Hitt, Certo, & Dalton, 2007; Nyberg, Fulmer, Gerhart, & Carpenter, 2010).

We argue that our effort is promising because separation across different management levels regarding decisions that involve strategic resources has been almost completely neglected by current managerial research (Sirmon, Hitt, Ireland, & Gilbert, 2011), although this type of situation is likely to frequently reoccur in any firm. In particular, following Sirmon, Hitt, and Ireland (2007), we focus on the separation between SHC structuration (i.e., decisions concerning human resources acquisition, development, and divestment) and SHC bundling (i.e., decisions concerning human resources combinations). Next, we investigate what occurs when the individual in charge of SHC bundling (henceforth, bundling), the agent, has a perspective that differs from that of the principal, who is concurrently in charge of SHC structuration (henceforth, structuration), because this situation may generate a P–A misalignment that damages the organization.

More specifically, the principal is interested in unit[1] performance sustainability over the mid- to long term (Jensen & Meckling, 1976), and he[2] therefore aims to renew the SHC endowment periodically, either before the contribution of current human resources to performance decreases (Berman, Down, & Hill, 2002; Katz, 1982), or to cope with employee mobility (Campbell, Coff, & Kryscynski, 2012; Lepak & Snell, 1999), or to appropriate rents (Makadok, 2001; Moliterno & Wiersema, 2007). To this end, the principal's structuration strategy requires new SHC to be adequately bundled and involved in team processes with current teammates to become valuable resources at the team level (Sirmon, Gove, & Hitt, 2008).

However, the uncertainty that characterizes new SHC's contribution to performance over the short term (Bauer, Morrison, & Callister, 1998; Chen, 2005; Chen & Klimoski, 2003; Coff, 1999) gives rise to the agent's concern – and potentially to a P–A conflict – a fortiori because the agent is risk averse (Jensen & Meckling, 1976) and preoccupied mostly with his unit's short-run performance. Consequently, the agent may not bundle new SHC as envisaged by the principal's structuration strategy.

In essence, whereas the principal conceives of the current unit performance as a premise for future unit success, the agent considers instead the unit's current success as the basis for his own future career, which will not necessarily occur in the same unit. Thus, the agent will not make risky decisions if he is uncertain that he will benefit. This phenomenon suggests that the agent may undertake bundling tactics that are not aligned with the principal's structuration strategy; for example, the SHC strategy decided by the principal may not be adequately implemented by the agent, or the SHC endowment chosen by the former might be used inappropriately by the latter.

To pursue our research goal, we conducted a study in the Italian "Serie A," the top-level professional football league, between 1960 and 1992. Sports settings are particularly suited to management research (see Day, Gordon, & Fink, 2012; Wolfe et al., 2005) because they frequently allow for the observation of phenomena of particular interest, such as managerial turnover (Pfeffer & Davis-Blake, 1986), resource management and sunk costs (Staw & Hoang, 1995), individual and collective skills (Berman et al., 2002; Shamsie & Mannor, 2013), resource management and value creation (Holcomb, Holmes, & Connelly, 2009), human resource bundling (Sirmon et al., 2008), and human resource acquisition and release (Moliterno & Wiersema, 2007). All these areas of interest are particularly relevant to our research.

We also clarify some boundary conditions. In particular, we concur with Eisenhardt (1989, p. 60), who maintains that the P–A approach "can be applied to employer–employee, lawyer–client, buyer–supplier, and other agency relationships." In addition, because we are interested in the separation among managerial decision levels, we assume, indifferently, that the principal is the firm's owner or top manager, whereas the agent is assumed to be a middle manager. Furthermore, although in many settings both principals and agents (i.e., both owners/CEOs and middle managers) have the power to make structuration and bundling decisions, we also clarify at this stage that there are nevertheless many contexts in which these tasks are clearly implemented separately. For example, in multiple-team organizations such as those in the software (Huckman, Staats, & Upton, 2009) or healthcare (Huckman & Pisano, 2006; Reagans, Argote, & Brooks, 2005) industries, a given owner/top manager may recruit professionals and allocate them to different groups, teams, business units, or operating theaters, where these resources are actually bundled by middle managers. In addition, several professional sport settings share this decision-making structure; for example, anecdotal evidence from Major League Baseball (Sexton & Lewis, 2003) indicates that the general manager (principal) is in charge of structuration, whereas the head coach (agent) is responsible for the starting line-up and game strategy. This approach is shared by the four most important football leagues in continental Europe (namely, the Italian, Spanish, French, and German leagues; Foot, 2007; Quelch, Nueno, & Knoop, 2004).

This chapter offers the following contributions. First, we explore the consequences of the separation of managerial decision-making functions regarding strategic resources by analyzing both the effect of the release of co-specialized SHC resources and SHC renewal decisions. Next, we argue that different decisional levels of SHC give rise to a P–A problem, thus extending the traditional domain of AT to SHC management. Finally, we address the P–A conflict and overcome the trade-off between the principal's risk tolerance and the agent's risk-averse attitude.

This chapter is organized as follows: the next section addresses the theoretical background and offers a set of hypotheses; that section is followed by the methodology section; next, results and discussion sections are presented; and, finally, we state our conclusions, highlight the limitations of our study, and propose directions for future research.

3.2   THE CHALLENGES OF STRATEGIC HUMAN CAPITAL RENEWAL

3.2.1   The Principal View of SHC Renewal

As highlighted in the second chapter, decisions aimed at developing specialized resources bring advantages to the organization. In particular, the processes aimed at fostering tacit knowledge sharing represent a fundamental activity in building and deploying co-specialized resources. Shared tacit knowledge, indeed, represents the basis for the development of collective routines that, in turn, are necessary to improve coordination among team members. Empirical evidence testifies that shared tacit knowledge leads to better performance and the reduction of time and errors at the team level (Berman et al., 2002; Reagans et al., 2005). However, several causes, both internal and external, may affect the availability of co-specialized resources, such as employee turnover, movements, promotions, and demotions (Lepak & Gowan, 2010).

Unfortunately, the extant literature has not adequately explored, to date, the consequences of the release of co-specialized knowledge resources when structuration decisions are taken separately (for instance, by a different individual) from bundling decisions, and has overlooked the related agency problems that can emerge.

In our study, we assume the principal is either the owner or a top manager in charge of structuration (i.e., human capital acquisition, development, and release) while the agent is the middle manager in charge of bundling decisions (i.e., deployment and exploitation of human capital). The principal's goal is to provide his unit with the appropriate resources to achieve sustainable performance over time. He has a mid- to long-term vision, which means that he is not indifferent to short-term results but is more focused on future performance in the medium term. In particular, he might be concerned that overall SHC performance might decrease over time. As argued in the previous chapter, this phenomenon may be caused by competence traps (Levitt & March, 1988), core capabilities evolving into core rigidities (Leonard-Barton, 1992 [2011]), cognitive inertia that hinders the recognition of opportunities and the need for change (Tripsas & Gavetti, 2000), knowledge ossification and conduct predictability (Berman et al., 2002), lack of synergy and/or diminishing productive capability (Moliterno & Wiersema, 2007).

As a result, the principal should be inclined to release current human resources and acquire new ones. Thus, from the perspective of risk taking and problem framing (Kahneman & Tversky, 1979; March & Shapira, 1987; Sitkin & Pablo, 1992), the principal sees SHC renewal as an opportunity not a threat. In addition, organizations do not make a one-time acquisition of relevant resources in the factor market (Barney, 1986; Cool, Dierickx, & Jemison, 1989); instead, they repeatedly seek potential gains from the acquisition and release of resources, including human resources (Moliterno & Wiersema, 2007).

Therefore, the principal plans to release current SHC and acquire new SHC. However, he must cope with several issues. For example, he must account for the fact that he is releasing firm-level expertise (i.e., he is releasing SHC co-specialization) while acquiring general, domain/ industry-level expertise (newcomers' experience in the industry). The former, which stems from a socially complex learning process, is unique, whereas the latter is more general and less uniquely suited to a particular context (Castanias & Helfat, 1991; Holcomb et al., 2009). Therefore, SHC release leads to the substitution of co-specialized knowledge with a general, unspecialized one. As a result, the release of co-specialized SHC is likely to negatively affect team-level coordination, since co-specialization among current human resources positively effects efficiency and effectiveness in terms, for example, of the amount of time required to execute a task and of a lower likelihood of making mistakes. This leads us to hypothesize that:

H1: There is a negative relationship between the release of co-specialized SHC and team performance.

In addition, the principal may wish to consider whether it is better to hire less domain-experienced SHC and develop their skills internally at the firm level or to hire more domain-experienced individuals who have previously developed their skills elsewhere (Lepak & Snell, 1999). Later, the principal may consider that new SHC performance may be uncertain upon joining a new workplace. This assessment has been empirically documented in research on situations in which newcomers suffer from performance uncertainty (Bauer et al., 1998; Chen, 2005; Chen & Klimoski, 2003; see also Rink, Kane, Ellemers, & Van der Vegt, 2013 for a review), which in turn might translate into their new employer's per-formance (Groysberg, Lee, & Nanda, 2008). Finally, because a positive return on new SHC acquisition is associated with their co-specialization with current employees (Huckman et al., 2009; Reagans et al., 2005), new SHC contribution to performance is contingent on such a co-specialization process and therefore is somehow temporally deferred.

In summary, these considerations imply that:

- it must be ascertained whether the new SHC expertise will affect the team's performance;
- it is not certain that the contribution of the new SHC will be positive, particularly in the short run; and
- some amount of time may be required before the new SHC is able to make positive contributions to performance.

Such implications characterize new SHC integration at the organizational level as a risky process, and although the principal may be willing to bear the risk associated with the integration of the new SHC, the agent may instead consider such integration to be highly detrimental both to his current results and his future career.

With respect to the implications of the new SHC acquisition, the principal – other things being equal and contingent on the human resources that he can afford – must take into account the level of experience (i.e., industry expertise) that the new individuals should have. In practical terms, the principal may opt for individuals with either high or low levels of expertise.

Industry- or domain-level expertise, which is represented by an individual's previous, cumulative experience in a given job context, is an important component of a firm's human capital endowment (Becker, 1964; Castanias & Helfat, 1991); however, its contribution to a given unit's performance is uncertain. On the one hand, some studies on such expertise suggest a positive effect on performance (Argote, 1999; Reagans et al., 2005), although its contribution may be influenced by workplace characteristics (Edmondson, Bohmer, & Pisano, 2001; Huckman & Pisano, 2006) and co-workers' variability (Huckman et al., 2009). On the other hand, other studies emphasize that industry-level expertise might be a double-edged sword because it may be associated with knowledge rigidity (Gilbert, 2005), conduct predictability (Berman et al., 2002), and diminished productivity (Moliterno & Wiersema, 2007). Thus, the acquisition of new SHC gives rise to conflicting options for the principal. We contextualize this dilemma in our research setting.

In the Italian Serie A football league, the principal (i.e., the team owner, aka *presidente*) plans to trade current players for the reasons discussed above and acquire new players. In particular, because experienced SHC already possess a set of the necessary skills (Lepak & Snell, 1999), the owner may want to replace a seasoned employee with an experienced player, because he does not want to take the risk associated with a young and inexperienced player. From this perspective, the principal may want to retain a substantial amount of domain expertise on his team by acquiring new assets characterized by a substantial experience, although this experience has been obtained in previous years when he worked for different organizations, because he believes that such previous experience would be beneficial for his team/unit. Thus, we propose the following hypothesis:

H2a: There is a positive relationship between new employees' domain expertise and team performance.

There could be, however, other concerns that affect a principal's decision, since he may fear that experienced newcomers have less commitment to the team/unit and that they may reduce their effort if their employment is not mutually satisfying (symbiotic employment; see Lepak & Snell, 1999). This occurs because experienced employees have previously developed their skills and may be less willing to engage in a new training process. Moreover, a substantial amount of previous experience may lead to inertia and rigidity and undermine the new employees' ability to learn and apply new practices. Therefore, the team/unit might benefit more by recruiting less experienced individuals with a higher commitment and willingness to learn and whose skill might be more easily co-specialized at the team level, over time, to become valuable and unique. Thus, we advance the following hypothesis:

H2b: There is a negative relationship between new employees' domain expertise and team performance.

Although an employee's domain experience represents an appropriate measure for appraising the expertise and the potential contribution of a new employee when he joins a new team, it falls short of capturing the nuances of the structuration decision concerning the renewal of SHC. Indeed, the experience and the contribution of the new SHC should be examined with respect to SHC experience released through structuration decisions. To account for this, we assess specifically the experience of newcomers, also taking account of the experience released through structuration decisions. This allows us to better understand whether an overall reduction in a team's SHC experience is likely to affect its results. In particular, we surmise that a decrease in a team's SHC general experience (assessed through employees' age), is likely to negatively affect performance, since younger employees are likely to be, other things being equal, less experienced and thus characterized by a lower level of domain expertise. Therefore, we hypothesize:

H3: A reduction in the amount of general experience of SHC negatively affects team performance.

Furthermore, the principal must consider the effect of newcomers' expertise on the performance of current SHC. Above we discussed the pros and cons of new employees' expertise when they join a new team/ unit, as these pros and cons represent the alternative options available to the principal in implementing his structuration strategy. However, when acquiring new SHC, the principal should also consider how current employees and newcomers will combine, that is, how their interaction will influence performance, because both new and current SHC will be used jointly in a given middle manager's bundling strategy.

This observation is consistent with claims from the resource-based view concerning resource integration and orchestration at the firm level (Peteraf, 1993; Sirmon et al., 2011). The previous literature, however, offers contrasting assumptions and evidence with regard to how SHC experience heterogeneity affects performance. More precisely, on the one hand, current SHC and newcomers might benefit from expertise heterogeneity because studies on group management suggest that heterogeneous group experience (in terms of members' expertise) positively affects performance (Hambrick, Cho, & Chen, 1996). For example, Berman et al. (2002, p. 19) maintain that from the viewpoint of experience heterogeneity, "the best-performing teams may have a mix of players with high tenure, who bring an understanding of both organizational and industry norms, and new players, who may bring a fresh perspective with youthful energy. The 1979–80 Los Angeles Lakers seemed to exemplify this mix, with the veterans Kareem Abdul-Jabbar and Jamaal Wilkes teamed with the rookie Earvin 'Magic' Johnson." On the other hand, other studies argue that a team benefits when newcomers and current players have similar domain or industry expertise, other things being equal, such that heterogeneity in that team's overall expertise is reduced. These results ensue because different levels of expertise among team members may lead to inconsistency and misunderstandings, whereas a similar level of expertise leads to better information processing (Reagans et al., 2005) and sense-making (Weick & Roberts, 1993), which positively affects results in turn. Thus, it may be better if newcomers and current employees have similar experience because homogeneity in team members' expertise seems to positively affect performance.

In summary, the managerial literature offers contrasting opinions and evidence concerning how (i.e., that is, either positively or negatively) expertise heterogeneity affects performance. To move beyond these contrasting stances, we argue that it is insufficient to observe overall team expertise heterogeneity subsequent to structuration decisions, because a given employee's expertise represents his domain expertise, that is, the level of general experience that he has acquired at the industry level. Instead, we decide to focus only on the heterogeneity among new players and, more precisely, with respect to heterogeneity of new players' expertise. This is because new employees' heterogeneity with respect to their expertise represents a double source of uncertainty in terms of their fruitful integration at the team level, since they are not only new to their teammates, but they also carry heterogeneous levels of industry expertise, too. Therefore, their integration at the team level with current teammates could be hindered by this double source of uncertainty. This leads us to hypothesize as follows:

H4: There is a negative relationship between the heterogeneity of new employees' expertise and team performance.

3.2.2 The Agent View and Potential Sources of P–A Conflict

The agent (i.e., the middle manager in charge of bundling) is aware that individuals perform better when they are co-specialized at the unit level. Research from the perspective of the resource-based (Barney, 1991; Peteraf, 1993), knowledge-based (Grant, 1996; Kogut & Zander, 1992), and capability-based (Amit & Schoemaker, 1993; Teece, Pisano, & Shuen, 1997 [2008]) views underscore the importance of human capital's tacit knowledge at the collective level, that is, knowledge that emanates from human capital co-specialization through complex, time-consuming, and socially embedded learning processes. Further studies testify that team familiarity and co-specialization foster team performance (Huckman et al., 2009; Reagans et al., 2005). However, SHC co-specialization can be achieved only if human resources are tied to the firm over time, committed to a unit's goal, and adequately involved (Lepak & Snell, 1999). In addition, Wang, He, and Mahoney (2009) have empirically observed that employees may choose not to co-specialize their skills if they have not received adequate incentives and consideration.

These studies clarify that valuable information – in the form of firm-specific, co-specialized employees' knowledge – is not always available (Fama & Jensen, 1983; Jensen & Meckling, 1976) and that once it has been generated it should be carefully preserved. Thus, the replacement of firm-level expertise (due to the loss of co-specialization subsequent to the release of traded players) by industry-level expertise (i.e., the not yet firm-specific skills of new players) represents an occurrence that engenders stress and uncertainty in the agent. In particular, the agent is not certain how newcomers will perform compared with the previously co-specialized traded players and – more precisely – he fears that newcomers' performance will be somewhat below the expected standard.

These concerns are consistent with studies on SHC interorganizational transfers, which have observed that even high-skilled newcomers may suffer from performance decline (Groysberg et al., 2008). Additionally, newcomers lack shared codes and languages (Nahapiet & Ghoshal, 1998) that are used among teammates (Shamsie & Mannor, 2013), and they do not have the advantage of familiarity with those colleagues (Huckman et al., 2009; Reagans et al., 2005). For example, Reagans et al. (2005) have observed a non-monotonic relationship (i.e., inverted-U shaped) between newcomers' experience with a team and the completion time of a surgical procedure. In essence, the presence of new team members who are domain experts negatively affects completion time until those individuals achieve an adequate level of co-specialization (i.e., firm-level expertise) with their teammates.

For all the above reasons, the agent considers the replacement of co-specialized individuals with new, unspecialized employees to be a threat, not an opportunity (Audia & Greve, 2006; Greve, 2003; Kahneman & Tversky, 1979; Sitkin & Pablo, 1992) because it is likely that the presence of new SHC will negatively affect team conduct and his present performance and future career prospects in turn. Therefore, the agent will not welcome the principal's structuration strategy to release current, co-specialized human resources – while concurrently acquiring new unspecialized individuals – and may not align his bundling choices (i.e., he will not bundle new SHC to an adequate extent) with the principal's strategy, who instead expects newcomers to be substantially utilized to achieve the principal's structuration strategy goals in the medium term.

The reasons behind the agent's behavior are self-interest and risk aversion, as observed by Audia and Greve (2006, p. 85), who maintain that, "perceptions of threat lead to psychological stress and anxiety, which restricts information processing and reduces behavioral flexibility. Finally, an inability to generate and consider risky alternatives makes decision makers rigid and risk averse." In sum, fearing that bundling new employees might negatively affect performance, the agent does not adequately bundle them. Consequently, his bundling decisions may not be aligned with the principal's SHC renewal strategy and may instead be oriented to curb the threat to his present and future career that the principal's structuration strategy represents. Moreover, previous human capital studies illustrate that the agent is often the type of employee who is generally more focused on his own career and less committed to the organization and who typically considers his relationship with the organization from a short-term perspective, that is, to be terminated when the cost of the partnership exceeds its benefit (a market-based configuration; see Lepak & Snell, 1999).

In sum, the agent may consider that the principal's structuration strategy (i.e., releasing co-specialized individuals and acquiring new employees) poses a risk to his present and future career. However, as an employee, either he must accept the *principal*'s decision or resign his position. Nevertheless, although the agent may appear to accept the principal's structuration strategy, he may make misaligned bundling decisions in practice that conflict with the structuration strategy because he expects a negative effect from bundling new employees. Thus, involving those individuals to a substantial extent would conflict with his self-interest and run counter to his risk aversion. To test agents' concerns about new SHC utilization, we hypothesize as follows:

H5: Bundling new employees with current employees negatively affects team performance.

In sum, the agent does not bundle new SHC because it would negatively affect performance, which may be highly detrimental to his present and future career. Therefore, although he might be confident in either the principal's luck or his ex ante picking capability (Barney, 1986; Makadok, 2001), the coach, most likely, will resist the principal's structuration strategy by means of his misaligned bundling choices and by underutilizing new SHC. Conversely, the principal needs the new human capital assets to be substantially bundled with current teammates, otherwise his structuration strategy is inadequately executed and therefore will fail to achieve the desired results, that is, the sustainability of the unit's performance in the medium to long term and not just over the short run. Therefore, it is of utmost importance that a coach bundles new SHC with current SHC because a misaligned bundling tactic may negatively impact the team structuration strategy by missing an opportunity to co-specialize newcomers and current employees.

The agent's concern is based on evidence that new SHC co-specialization at the team level requires some time (Reagans et al., 2005); however, by failing to adequately involve newcomers in the team processes, the agent hinders the expected effect of their integration on team performance. In addition, because newly acquired SHC that are not adequately involved in the team's processes may thereafter reduce their effort and commitment (symbiotic employment: Lepak & Snell, 1999; see also Wang et al., 2009), the lower bundling of new SHC with current teammates may mean the longer time it will take before new members' contribution to performance is observed. In sum, because the positive impact of newcomers on performance is expected to have a temporal lag since they must co-specialize their skills at the team level, inadequate bundling of newcomers constrains their expected future contributions. Finally, it should be noted that newcomers who have not shared prior training with current, co-specialized teammates are likely to suffer from lack of coordination (Reagans et al., 2005) and sense-making (Weick & Roberts, 1993), since it is likely that it takes time for newcomers to fully understand existing team-level codes and languages (Nahapiet & Ghoshal, 1998). Thus, newly acquired employees require a certain amount of training and field experience with their new teammates before their knowledge of team mechanisms allows them to achieve positive levels of performance. To test whether an agent's concern is empirically grounded, we therefore test whether negative short-term results are likely to increase the probability of a middle manager lay-off. Thus, we hypothesize as follows:

H6: Negative short-term performance increases the likelihood of middle manager lay-off.

3.3 RESEARCH METHODOLOGY

3.3.1 Setting

The Italian Serie A professional football league represents a competitive context that is similar to several business settings. In the Italian Serie A, there are typically two decision makers: the team owner (*presidente*) and the team's coach (*allenatore*), a middle manager. The owner sets the team's strategy: he hires a coach and selects a roster of players. The team's coach acts at a lower decisional level than the owner. In particular, he is in charge of training players and responsible for bundling the starting line-up, although he is not in charge of players' acquisition and release (Brera, 1975; Foot, 2007; Sconcerti, 2009). The starting line-up is the best resource combination that the coach is able to organize, and a coach typically bundles the best resources at the beginning of each match that suits his preferred strategy. Obviously, to remain in charge and avoid being fired, a coach must win as many games as possible and also attempt to demonstrate his contribution through a recognizable set of game tactics.

Because of the high level of popularity of and *endemic* passion for football across virtually every tier of Italian society (Brera, 1975; Foot, 2007; Sconcerti, 2009), coaching a football team in the Italian Serie A is a highly demanding job. Furthermore, at the end of every season there are many player trades among virtually all the teams. In addition, daily widespread media coverage by three sports-dedicated newspapers (i.e., *La Gazzetta dello Sport*, *Corriere dello Sport*, and *Tuttosport*) – in addition to the sports section of every national and regional newspaper – places coaches, management, and players under a magnifying glass. These features make the Serie A a highly appropriate setting for exploring our P–A argument concerning SHC renewal decisions.

3.3.2 Sample and Data

We collected data on a game-day basis between the 1960–61 and 1991–92 seasons. We gathered our data from two main sources: the *Enciclopedia Panini del Calcio Italiano, 1960-2000* (2000) and the *Almanacco Illustrato del Calcio* (years 1960–91). Both sources are published by Panini, which is widely considered to be the most authoritative and accurate source of information about Italian football. Additionally, we explored several issues from the 1960–92 archives of *La Gazzetta dello Sport*, which is the oldest and most widely distributed sports news-paper in Italy. We also interviewed several experts, and we explored the database of the Rec.Sport.Soccer Statistics Foundation (RSSSF).[3]

Specifically, our sample consists of data on players, coaches, and team performances from the 1960–61 through the 1991–92 seasons. Because our unit of analysis is the football team, data on players and coaches is used to construct measures at the team level. Taking into account changes in the composition of the Serie A teams list over the years (i.e., the fact that teams upgrade from and downgrade to Serie B during our sample period), there are a total of 43 teams in the dataset.[4] In particular, from the 1960–61 through the 1966–67 seasons, and from the 1988–89 through the 1991–92 seasons, 18 teams played in the Serie A, whereas from the 1967–68 through the 1987–88 seasons, only 16 teams played in that league. Therefore, our sample contains 534 team-year observations across 32 years (i.e., football seasons).

Moreover, to construct variables at different levels of analysis (i.e., individual, team firm), we used the dataset in which the game-day, not the year, is the time unit. Depending on the number of teams competing in Serie A each season, the number of matches per year changes. Therefore, because all the teams play one another twice, once at "home" and once "away" (i.e., a double round-robin format), the total game-days were 34 for the time periods in which there were 18 teams, thus providing 612 observations per year, multiplied by 11 seasons, which results in 6732 observations. For the time period in which there were 16 teams (seasons 1967–68 through 1987–88), the total number of match-days was 30, which is multiplied by 16 teams and 480 observations per year and in turn multiplied by 21 seasons and thus results in 10 080 overall observations. The overall total number of observations is 16 812.

3.3.3   Dependent Variables

To test our hypotheses, we use three different dependent variables:

* *Season wins*. This is measured through total wins at the end of the season. This measurement is similar to the measures of performance utilized by other studies exploring sports settings (Berman et al., 2002; Holcomb et al., 2009; Pfeffer & Davis-Blake, 1986; Sirmon et al., 2008).

- *Net goal score.* The difference between scored and conceded goals, calculated at the end of the season. It is an important performance measure because in the time window of our study this performance indicator was employed as a tie-breaker rank measure in case of a tie rank position at the end of the season, since the Italian Serie A league has no post-season play-offs. Only in case of a tie rank at the first position is there a mandatory, one-shot, play-off game. This happened just once in the history of Italian football, in 1966.
- *New coach.* This is a dummy variable equal to 1 when a coach is removed from his position during the current season, and 0 otherwise. This variable allows us to assess whether the coach is replaced during the season due to short-term results. If negative short-term results may instigate a coach's replacement, he will have no advantage in pursuing bundling choices that could pay off in the middle term but could negatively affect short-term results. A premature substitution on a team's bench during the season is indeed likely to have negative consequences on the reputation of a coach and on his future chances of obtaining a new job, not only in the context of Serie A, but also in the context of minor leagues (Serie B or even Serie C), and to receive an adequate payment fee.

3.3.4   Independent Variables

- *Released players' co-specialization.* We draw from Reagans et al. (2005) to calculate this measure. For each pair of players on a team, we first consider the number of times that they have been bundled together in a given season. Next, we sum across pairs on a team that include at least one released player and divide by team size. The formula is:

$$\sum_{i=1}^{R} \sum_{j=1}^{N} CKij/N(N-1)/2$$

$CKij$ is the number of times that player i (i.e., the released player) has been bundled with player j (whether that player was a released player, or whether he remained on the team), which we define as the co-specialized SHC at the pair level, where R is the number of released players at the end of the season and N is team size. This measure gauges the amount of co-specialized knowledge developed during the previous season and released at the beginning of the current season.

- *New players' expertise*. We calculate this variable to take account of new players' expertise, that is, their domain/industry expertise. We first compute the total number of career games up to the previous season (as a member of the starting line-up); then, following Dirks (2000), we multiply this number by $(1 - (1/N))$, where N is the number of seasons the player had been in Serie A. This measure demonstrates that a large number of games played over a large number of seasons can be considered a stronger measure of expertise than a large number of games played over a smaller number of seasons.

- *Green ratio*. This is the mean age of players released at the end of the previous season divided by the mean age of the players acquired at the beginning of the current season. This variable allows us to grasp the strategy underlying the choices of structuration, which can be more oriented to the composition of a young team on which to build skills or aimed at maintaining the same structure in terms of experience.

- *Standard deviation of new players' expertise*. This is the standard deviation of new players' expertise. This variable allows us to capture the level of heterogeneity subsequent to structuration decision, that is, after the principal has made his renewal decisions concerning strategic human resources.

- *Bundling of new players*. This variable is the mean of the number of new players lined up per game-day during the season. This variable assesses whether the coach (i.e., the middle manager) involves new strategic resources in the team at the end to co-specialize with those resources that already make up the team or pursues opportunistic behaviors aimed at not having negative results in the short term while forgoing long-term goals.

- *Season losses*. This is the number of losses suffered by a given team in a season. We use this variable to assess the effect of the number of losses on the likelihood of the coach's replacement.

3.3.5 Additional Control Variables

- *Team historical average rank*. This variable is the mean count of the positions obtained by a given team in all the previous seasons and is meant to control whether a team's rank in previous seasons influences its ability to gain points in subsequent years. We multiply that count by minus one (–1) to ensure that the best teams are associated with the highest values and that the worst teams are associated with the lowest values, which makes the regression results more intuitively interpretable.

• *Players' quality.* To gauge this variable, we begin by considering the quality of players at the individual level, that is, at the single-player level. First, we count the number of games played by a given player for each season, then we multiply that count by the team's total points at the end of that season, and finally we divide that number by the player's age. We provide the rationale for this measure in the following. Because Italian football is a tremendously selective and competitive setting, it is difficult for a Serie A player to be in the starting line-up continuously (Brera, 1975; Sconcerti, 2009). Therefore, a player who plays a high number of games per season is a highly qualified professional football player. Furthermore, drawing on studies addressing the contribution of human capital to performance, which take into account work experience weighted by the quality of the employers and other features of human capital (Campbell et al., 2012; Huckman & Pisano, 2006; Ployhart & Moliterno, 2011), a player on a Serie A top-ranked team must be considered of higher quality than a player on a lower-level team.

Finally, we consider that even the quality of highly qualified players decreases due to age. We count this value per year, not including the current season; in addition, we carried out validation procedures. We apply this measure to gauge the quality of each new player and then we calculate the mean value of new players' quality.

• *Coaches' relative tenure.* This variable is the number of years that a given coach has been with a given team lagged by one year to avoid endogeneity concerns.

3.3.6   Model Specification

We employ longitudinal regressions to test our hypotheses. Our observation unit is the team-year. We run a preliminary Durbin-Wu-Hausman test to ascertain the need for a fixed effect at the team level (i.e., the existence of a correlation between the fixed effect and other covariates). More specifically, we use a panel fixed-effect model through Stata 15 SE (command: xtreg, fe) to account for firm-specific unobserved heterogeneity (Bowen & Wiersema, 1999; Greene, 2003). The persistency in the team results that we observed in the Italian Serie A football league allows us to address autocorrelation by including the first lag of the control variable. However, we take account of these occurrences in our analyses. It seems that covariance in our data sample may be due to the presence of certain potential occurrences such as, for example, teams' characteristics.

Thus, we specified cluster standard error. Therefore, the fixed-effects model is given by the following equation (in this model *i* is the team and *t* is the year):

$$Y_{it} = \beta_0 + \beta_j \, X_{i,t-1} + \beta_k \, X_{i,t} + a_i + u_{i,t}$$

where y_{it} is the dependent variable, β_j is the vector of coefficients, $X_{i,t-1}$ is the vector of predictors (calculate at time t – 1), β_k is the vector of coefficients, $X_{i,t}$ is the vector of predictors (calculate at time t), a_i are the team fixed effects, and $u_{i,t}$ is the error term.

3.4   RESULTS

Table 3.1 reports descriptive statistics and correlation analysis; Table 3.2 (Models 1–10) reports the results of our hypotheses testing on the effects of structuration decision on dependent variables (H1–H4).

Table 3.2 (Models 1 and 2) reports a baseline with control variables and season win and net goal score, respectively, as dependent variables. H1 predicted that releasing SHC co-specialization negatively affects team performance. The coefficient on the season wins in Model 3 is negative and statistically significant ($\beta = -0.229$; $p < 0.001$). Model 4 tests the effect of releasing SHC co-specialization on a different performance measure, net goal score. The coefficient for releasing SHC co-specialization in Model 4 is negatively and statistically significant ($\beta = -0.687$; $p < 0.001$). Thus, both Models 3 and 4 provided support for H1.

Models 5 and 6 explore the consequence of the principal's structuration strategy and clarifies the relevance of newcomers' domain expertise and their impact on both season win and net goal score. We were initially agnostic regarding whether newcomers' expertise could exert a positive or a negative effect on a team's performance (respectively, H2a and H2b). Furthermore, we maintain that new expertise joining a given team should be examined with respect to its general renewal strategy by assessing the relationship between experience released in terms of players' mean age, and experience acquired, measured as mean age of new players (H3). Our

Table 3.1   *Means, standard deviations, and correlations*

	Mean	S.D.	Min	Max	(1)	(2)	(3)	(4)	(5)	(6)	(7)	(8)
(1) Players' quality	94.35	53.03	1.38	272.08								
(2) Team historical average rank (t − 1)	-8.52	3.77	-18	-1	0.666 0.000							
(3) Coaches' relative tenure	2.14	1.6	1	10	0.263 0.000	0.287 0.000						
(4) Released employees' co-specialization	7.13	4.34	0.09	23.94	-0.438 0.000	-0.444 0.000	-0.042 -0.416					
(5) New players' expertise	9.32	10.41	0	97.5	0.359 0.000	0.093 -0.045	-0.061 -0.24	-0.014 -0.763				
(6) Green ratio	1.08	0.12	0.8	1.6	-0.012 -0.81	0.054 -0.268	0.029 -0.575	-0.023 -0.639	-0.163 -0.001			
(7) Standard new players' expertise	10.61	11	0	56.33	0.285 0.000	0.038 -0.436	-0.044 -0.424	0.103 -0.034	0.848 0.000	-0.177 -0.001		
(8) Bundling of new players	3.82	2.41	0.3	11.03	-0.504 0.000	-0.506 0.000	-0.082 -0.109	0.849 0	-0.05 -0.278	-0.146 -0.003	0.061 -0.212	
(9) Season losses	9.81	4.21	0	24	-0.575 0.000	-0.586 0.000	-0.223 0.000	0.327 0.000	-0.126 -0.006	0.049 -0.318	-0.098 -0.044	0.377 0.000

Table 3.2   Regression analyses of structuration choices on team performance

	Model 1	(Model 2	Model 3	Model 4	Model 5	Model 6	Model 7	Model 8	Model 9	Model 10
	win_caricati	diff_reti_caricati	win_caricati	diff_reti_caricati	win_caricati	diff_reti_caricati	win_caricati	diff_reti_caricati	win_caricati	diff_reti_caricati
Players' quality	0.0000580	0.000312	0.000177	0.000599	0.000219	0.00107	-0.000000462	0.000148	0.000486	0.00102
	(0.000243)	(0.000954)	(0.000245)	(0.00108)	(0.000238)	(0.00110)	(0.000244)	(0.000923)	(0.000354)	(0.00141)
Team historical average rank (t-1)	0.343	0.736	0.655***	2.520***	0.333	0.625	0.403	0.903	0.296	0.597
	(0.254)	(0.737)	(0.0753)	(0.299)	(0.253)	(0.752)	(0.276)	(0.807)	(0.251)	(0.765)
Coaches' relative tenure	0.0864	0.603	0.181	0.685†	0.0678	0.540	0.0869	0.605	0.146	1.139**
	(0.114)	(0.446)	(0.115)	(0.415)	(0.104)	(0.434)	(0.108)	(0.424)	(0.0861)	(0.328)
Released employees' co-specialization			-0.229***	-0.687**						
			(0.0649)	(0.212)						
New players' expertise					-0.0191	-0.0912				
					(0.0235)	(0.0611)				
Green ratio							-4.423**	-12.44*		
							(1.285)	(4.614)		
Standard new players' expertise									-0.0456†	-0.0710
									(0.0229)	(0.0684)
_cons	13.07***	7.053	16.38***	23.64***	12.89***	5.589	18.45***	22.18†	12.04***	3.296
	(2.186)	(6.643)	(1.062)	(4.653)	(2.162)	(6.786)	(3.475)	(11.21)	(2.364)	(7.241)

	Model 1	(Model 2	Model 3	Model 4	Model 5	Model 6	Model 7	Model 8	Model 9	Model 10
	win_caricati	diff_reti_caricati	win_caricati	diff_reti_caricati	win_caricati	diff_reti_caricati	win_caricati	diff_reti_caricati	win_caricati	diff_reti_caricati
R^2	0.012	0.014			0.017	0.022	0.037	0.033	0.041	0.042
N	381	381	381	381	369	369	381	381	330	330

Note: Standard errors in parentheses.† $p < 0.10$, * $p < 0.05$, ** $p < 0.01$, *** $p < 0.001$.

findings do not support H2a or H2b, because the impact of new players' expertise on performance reported a non-significant result (Model 5: β = -0.0191; $p > 0.1$; Model 6: $\beta = -0.0912$; $p > 0.1$). We empirically observe that the green ratio (i.e., the ratio between release players' mean age and acquired players' mean age) affects both the ability to win a match and the ability to score goals (respectively: Model 7: $\beta = -4.423$; $p < 0.01$ and Model 8: $\beta = -12.44$; $p < 0.05$). This result further confirms our agnosticism about the effect of newcomers' expertise on performance because we should consider the general strategy implemented by top managers. More precisely, when top managers aim to reduce the amount of team experience there is a negative effect on performance, at least in the short term. We also observe that the standard deviation of new players' expertise affects the ability to win, measured through season win (Model 9: $\beta = -0.0456$; $p < 0.05$), while its effect was not significant on the other performance measure, net goal score. Thus, we found weak support for H4, which maintained a negative relationship between heterogeneity of new players' expertise and team performance. With regard to Model 10, we did not find a significant result concerning the effect of SD of new players' expertise on "net goal score," thus we conclude that new human capital heterogeneity does not affect the observed performance.

Next, we report our results with regard to the agent perspective on new SHC utilization and the root of the P–A conflict (Table 3.3).

Table 3.3, Models 1 and 2 report control models with the performance measures of our study – respectively, season wins and net goal score. Models 3 and 4 report the negative relationship between bundling of new players and performance on a team-year results basis (H5, Model 3: $\beta = -0.564$; $p < 0.001$; Model 4: $\beta = -2.045$; $p < 0.001$). These results provide support for the hypothesis that maintained that the deployment of new resources leads to negative organizational results, at least in the short term.

Since our findings confirm that bundling new players reduces the likelihood of winning a game (H5), we also tested whether losing games (gauged through the number of losses in the season) affects the likelihood of an anticipated replacement of the coach during the season.

Table 3.4 reports the results of the logit analysis (in particular, Model 1 reports a baseline of controls); Model 2 reports the marginal effects of losing game on the probability of anticipated replacement of the coach during the season (Model 2: $\beta = 0.136$; $p < 0.001$), thus supporting the agent's risk aversion as concerns new SHC utilization.

Table 3.3   *Regression analyses for bundling decisions on team performance*

	Model 1 Season wins	Model 2 Net goal score	Model 3 Season wins	Model 4 Net goal score
Quality players	0.0000580	0.000312	−0.000242	−0.000775
	(0.000243)	(0.000954)	(0.000238)	(0.000818)
Team historical average rank (t − 1)	0.343	0.736	0.260	0.433
	(0.254)	(0.737)	(0.222)	(0.612)
Coaches' relative tenure (t − 1)	0.0864	0.603	0.111	0.691
	(0.114)	(0.446)	(0.110)	(0.429)
Bundling of new players			−0.564***	−2.045***
			(0.135)	(0.354)
_cons	13.07***	7.053	14.72***	13.03*
	(2.186)	(6.643)	(1.757)	(5.714)
R^2	0.012	0.014	0.056	0.069
N	381	381	381	381

Note: Standard errors in parentheses.† $p < 0.10$, * $p < 0.05$, ** $p < 0.01$, *** $p < 0.001$.

Table 3.4   *Logistic regression analysis on the likelihood of coach replacement/firing*

	Model 1 New coach	Model 2 New coach
Players' quality	−0.00283	−0.000577
	(0.00309)	(0.00321)
Team historical average rank (t − 1)	−0.0376	−0.0526
	(0.116)	(0.117)
Coaches' relative tenure (t − 1)	0.0620	0.0737
	(0.0713)	(0.0731)
lose_tot		0.136***
		(0.0412)
R^2		
N	356	356

Taken together, these findings support the negative effect of new SHC utilization on team performance, which confirms that the agent's risk aversion is justified with respect to the non-integration of newcomers at the team level.

3.5   UNDERSTANDING THE RELATIONSHIP BETWEEN SHC RENEWAL AND ORGANIZATIONAL PERFORMANCE

The separation of resource management decisions across different managerial levels has received limited research effort to date (Sirmon et al., 2011). Therefore, in this chapter, we have explored this issue with respect to SHC. Our findings confirm that such separation may represent a critical issue because it can engender a P–A conflict centered upon both SHC release and renewal. More precisely, the *principal*, who is in charge of SHC structuration (i.e., decisions concerning the acquisition, development, and release of SHC), may need to replace (renew) SHC for a number of reasons, and he thus considers SHC replacement to be an opportunity. Conversely, the *agent*, who is in charge of SHC bundling (i.e., decisions concerning SHC utilization and combination), fears that replacing co-specialized human resources will negatively affect the team's short-run performance and he thus believes it is a threat to his present and future career.

We are confident that our findings make valuable contributions to both the SHC and P–A literature. With respect to the former, we clarify some underexplored research questions about the *principal*'s SHC structuration strategy, particularly with regard to the need to pay attention to integrating newcomers with current co-specialized teammates. With respect to the latter, we highlight why and how the P–A conflict unfolds and extend the reasons for the P–A conflict from a purely economic-financial perspective to a human capital, knowledge-based perspective, which is an insight that has been largely overlooked in AT research (Dalton et al., 2007; Nyberg et al., 2010; Tosi, Werner, Katz, & Gomez-Mejia, 2000), but which is consistent with new developments in the theory of the firm (Rajan & Zingales, 2001).

What emerges from our findings is a negative effect of the release of SHC co-specialization on team performance. Because this can be due to several causes concerning both voluntary and involuntary occurrences of human capital replacement, the principal must be prepared to cope with this negative effect through an adequate and planned reconstruction of the SHC and its co-specialization. Our study reveals that the *principal* must pay attention to, mainly, homogeneity of experience of new players rather than to individual experience level of new players.

In addition, our agnosticism regarding the contribution of new players' experience was justified, since we empirically observed that the effect of new SHC expertise on performance was non-significant. Therefore, we investigated whether the heterogeneity of SHC expertise affected performance and find a marginal support for this hypothesis. Taken together, these results allow us to move beyond the conflicting evidence supporting either a positive (Hambrick et al., 1996) or a negative (Berman et al., 2002) effect of overall team domain expertise on performance. More precisely, we argue that this variable is theoretically misleading because it measures whether heterogeneity in domain expertise at the overall team level (i.e., current players plus newcomers) influences performance, since it is generally agreed that firm-level expertise of current SHC obtained through co-specialization (Lepak & Snell, 1999; Reagans et al., 2005) is more significant than current SHC industry expertise. In addition, we have observed that replacing experienced employees with younger newcomers negatively affects organizational results. In particular, our study empirically demonstrates that a decrease in the overall experience available at the unit/team level, at least in the short term, damages a given unit/team's performance.

In sum, at least in the Italian Serie A, it seems there is no reason to bundle newcomers with current teammates, which therefore also raises concerns about the SHC renewal strategy as a whole. We argue that this issue is underexplored in the SHC literature (Lepak & Snell, 1999; Ployhart & Moliterno, 2011), with few exceptions (Groysberg et al., 2008). Instead, our findings invite the managers in charge of structuration and bundling to jointly plan a strategy that envisions new SHC recruitment and integration with future teammates within a shared SHC renewal policy, which represents a concern also shared by research on team receptivity to newcomers (Chen, 2005; Rink et al., 2013).

We observed that bundling new SHC might even negatively affect performance, which is an issue that raises the *agent*'s concerns. This finding is relevant because it shifts the object of the P–A contention and sheds new light on the *agent*'s reasons for gaming the *principal*'s strategy because the *agent* fears that new SHC integration will undermine team performance, which can damage his present results and future career. Our findings further support the correctness of the *agent*'s risk aversion by empirically observing that the number of losses increases the likelihood of being replaced early in the season.

To our knowledge, this research is one of the first to explore preferences and actions, instead of economic and financial inducements, as a source of P–A misalignment; in particular, our study is most likely the first to address the P–A conflict from the viewpoint of human capital and knowledge resources. Because knowledge resources have largely been neglected in the AT domain – in spite of the fact that the contribution of such resources to firm success is considered even more important than financial resources (Rajan & Zingales, 2001) – we argue that this insight is valuable for future research into this domain.

Our conclusions are also reinforced by evidence that the *agent*'s alignment is fundamental to an effective SHC structuration strategy; because new SHC performance suffers from a temporal lag, the less the new players are involved during the current year (i.e., misaligned bundling), the more their co-specialization with current teammates will be delayed, and the higher the risk of failure for the structuration strategy. However, from the *agent*'s perspective, it is irrational and against his self-interest to bundle new SHC to any substantial extent if he expects that new SHC will have a negative effect on performance.

Furthermore, even considering that a substantial utilization of such resources would be beneficial with some temporal lag (that is, the next season), the coach may not be willing to take the risk of integrating new SHC if he is not sure whether he would benefit from that risky decision.[5] Although a lower level of integration of new SHC should positively affect current-year performance, and thus be a positive occurrence for both the *agent* and the *principal*, this approach could cause a negative result for the *principal*'s structuration strategy because the purpose of the latter is to renew the SHC competitive potential over the medium to long term, and not merely for the current year.

Thus, a misaligned bundling that entrenches loyal veterans and excludes new SHC will be detrimental to the team's future results and will undermine the entire structuration strategy because the time-deferred effect of new SHC integration would be hindered or even nullified. We argue that this finding also contributes to extend the AT domain towards the exploration of the returns associated with human capital resources decisions and the investigation of conflicts surrounding such important resources.

Finally, our findings carry interesting managerial implications, too. In particular, we argue that the owner–coach conflict over the (mis)utilization of new SHC could be harnessed through the use of an agreement that includes incentives aimed at fostering consistent utilization of new SHC. We argue, however, that to pursue this goal the owner should not use incentives linked to the rate of new SHC utilization. Instead, we maintain that it would be more effective to reassure the middle manager through the use of an agreement reflecting a medium-term orientation (i.e., an explicit guarantee that there will be no repercussions due to poor performance resulting from substantially utilizing new SHC) aimed at excluding an early-season firing/replacement. This arrangement could encourage the coach to accept the risk of a low-performance season due to new SHC integration, whereas the owner may be glad to see his structuration strategy adequately implemented by the middle manager. Indeed, a well-implemented co-specialization of new SHC is a *sine qua non* for future performance and also for the future divestment of valuable SHC – for example, for purposes of rent appropriation – an achievement that cannot be reached without adequate new SHC bundling. We argue that such arrangements would also be a useful way to overcome the trade-off between incentives and monitoring (Tosi et al., 1997; Zajac & Westphal, 1994).

Obviously, our study is not without limitations; however, we are confident that those limitations may represent useful directions for future research. A first limitation is represented by the generalizability of our findings to settings other than sports. We argue that our findings may be usefully applied to business settings because top and middle managers may have diverging opinions about new SHC utilization; however, each must cope with the consequences of SHC renewal. This result is consistent, for example, with Huckman et al.'s (2009) study of the software industry, which involved the phenomenon of team managers' bias against specific team members. Further research about the phenomenon that is the subject of our investigation might corroborate and extend our insights. Another limitation of this study is represented by the limited set of information concerning SHC characteristics in our dataset; although we argue that our study would benefit from a broader set of SHC features, as suggested by Ployhart and Moliterno (2011), unfortunately such information was not available to us. Nevertheless, we believe that including other SHC features related to the issue explored in this book represents a fruitful direction for future research.

3.6   CONCLUSION

To date, P–A studies have primarily focused on financial resources as a means of achieving P–A alignment, while almost completely neglecting the role of SHC (i.e., human capital and knowledge resources) for pursuing such alignment. In this study, we have empirically observed that SHC may also represent a contentious issue for *principal* structuration strategy and for *agent* bundling decisions and that misaligned SHC bundling may have negative repercussions for the firm. We also observe, however, that such conflict is not unavoidable and that a mutually satisfactory agreement may be achieved through the use of an adequate arrangement that considers how other inducements (that is, not the traditional incentives) may adequately address the *agent* misaligned bundling issue.

NOTES

1. In this book, we use the terms unit, business unit, firm, and organization interchangeably.
2. We adopt "he/his" throughout the book for the sake of clarity, because our empirical setting is that of a male professional sport, notwithstanding the fact that our theoretical argument applies equally to any gender.
3. See http://www.rsssf.com.
4. 1. Ascoli; 2. Atalanta; 3. Avellino; 4. Bari; 5. Bologna; 6. Brescia; 7. Cagliari; 8. Catania; 9. Catanzaro; 10. Cesena; 11. Como; 12. Cremonese; 13. Empoli; 14. Fiorentina; 15. Foggia; 16. Genoa; 17. Internazionale; 18. Juventus; 19. L.R. Vicenza; 20. Lazio; 21. Lecce; 22. Lecco; 23. Mantova; 24. Messina; 25. Milan; 26. Modena; 27. Napoli; 28. Padova; 29. Palermo; 30. Parma; 31. Perugia; 32. Pescara; 33. Pisa; 34. Pistoiese; 35. Roma; 36. Sampdoria; 37. Spal; 38. Ternana; 39. Torino; 40. Udinese; 41. Varese; 42. Venezia; 43. Verona.
5. It would indeed be paradoxical if a coach were to be fired because of poor performance due to new SHC bundling, and that such resources would perform nicely during the subsequent year, thanks to a bundling choice made by the former coach that was continued by the new coach.

4. Get the most from your most important asset: A conceptual and managerial model for harnessing the value of strategic human capital

4.1 THE INNER VALUE OF STRATEGIC HUMAN CAPITAL: DEVELOPING COMPETENCES THROUGH SKILLED HUMAN RESOURCES DEPLOYMENT

The purpose of this book is an ambitious one, since it aims to overcome a number of inconsistencies either at the theoretical or at the methodological level with regard to human capital, their development as a firm/unit level resource, and their actual contribution to organizational overall performance.

In the previous chapters we have highlighted why extant research in different domains omitted to identify some relevant theoretical as well as methodological issues. At the same time, we have provided a number of conceptual insights and empirical results, along with several theoretical contributions with regard to, respectively, the relevance of shared experience in the context of co-specialized human capital, heterogeneity of human capital assets, and the role of the meso-managerial level in the quest for human capital-based competitive advantage.

Drawing from these contributions, in this chapter we complete our analysis regarding the development of human capital as a resource at the unit/firm level, and subsequently we provide a conceptual model for harnessing human capital and helping scholars and managers to understand in detail how this highly relevant resource contributes to firms' success.

First, we focus our contribution on the importance of the meso-managerial level in human capital management and deployment and clarify why its neglect by extant studies is a critical fallacy by observing that the two major disciplines interested in this important resource (that is, strategic management and human resources/organizational behavior) failed to understand how this main component (individuals' knowledge, skills, abilities, and other characteristics – KSAOs – at the unit/firm level) is actually conveyed to the collective, higher-order level, which constitutes a major area of inconsistency.

To address this inconsistency, we maintain that it should be first investigated why the above disciplines overlooked how human capital components (i.e., KSAOs) are treated in their respective conceptual frameworks and research agenda. Subsequently, we advance a conceptual framework describing how human capital evolves from a collection of individuals' KSAOs into a collective, higher-order resource at the unit/firm level, thanks to the introduction of a meso level in the conceptual framework of human capital resources. Figure 4.1 illustrates succinctly the major areas of ambiguity and fallacy in the context of strategic management and human resources/organizational behavior (HR/OB).

In the remainder of this section, we clarify why both disciplines failed to understand the actual dynamic that transforms individuals' KSAOs into organizational-level, higher-order competences and capabilities.

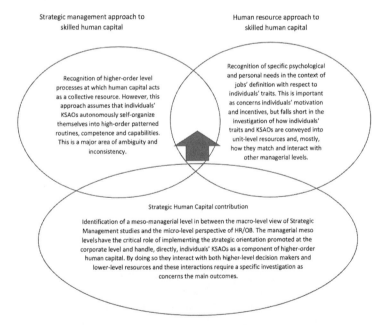

Figure 4.1   Strategic human capital approach and contributions

In the strategic management domain, an established research tradition has advanced the relevance of distributed competences and capabilities acting at the organizational level by means of higher-order principles and values (Nelson & Winter, 1982; Penrose, 1959). This tradition has been subsequently developed by studies on the resource-based view of the firm (Barney, 1991; Peteraf, 1993; Wernerfelt, 1984), and in the competence- (Kogut & Zander, 1992; Prahalad & Hamel, 1990 [2007]) and capability-based approaches (Peteraf & Maritan, 2007; Teece, Pisano, & Shuen, 1997 [2008]).

Common to these theoretical frameworks is a holistic view of human capital-based higher-order resources, in the context of which individuals acting at different organizational levels convey their KSAOs to compound higher-order patterned resources, based on routines and distributed knowledge at the organizational level. However, notwithstanding this elegant and stylized theoretical framework, several critiques have been raised with respect to the way higher-order resources should be operationalized and assessed (Peteraf, DiStefano, & Verona, 2013; Ployhart & Moliterno, 2011; Priem & Butler, 2001). Furthermore, we maintain that another major area of ambiguity should be clarified, specifically concerning the way individuals' KSAOs are conveyed into higher-order resources at the unit/firm level. More precisely, the resource-, competence-, and capability-based approaches took for granted that individuals' KSAOs are always available and that they fit smoothly into higher-order processes.

However, studies in the context of learning and shared experience (Berman, Down, & Hill, 2002; Groysberg, Lee, & Nanda, 2008; Reagans, Argote, & Brooks, 2005) empirically observed that the contribution of individuals' KSAOs to organizational higher-order resources and performance is not always positive and, that, under specific contingencies, it may even be negative. This is a first area of ambiguity stemming from the strategic management literature. And there is a second fallacy too. More precisely, studies in this tradition assume implicitly that higher-order competences and capabilities have the peculiar property of autonomous formation and self-organization and deployment. Unfortunately, extant research in the context of organizational learning conceptually maintained and empirically observed that organizational higher-order resources require specific organizational processes, otherwise they are likely to incur negative results (Edmondson, Bohmer, & Pisano, 2001; Huckman & Pisano, 2006).

This conceptual void requires further theoretical development especially with respect to the need for a meso-managerial level in between the macro-managerial and the micro-operative levels. Managerial meso-level competences and capabilities are of the utmost importance since they bear the responsibility of implementing the strategic view decided at the top managerial level, and their collaboration in the implementation stage of a firm's strategy is a necessary (although not sufficient) condition for firms' success. However, meso-level managerial cooperation can neither be taken for granted nor overlooked, as we have observed in previous chapters and will explain in further detail in the following sections of this chapter.

With regard, instead, to the human resource/organization behavior approach, almost in a parallel fashion with the strategic management literature, scholars and researchers endeavored to investigate individuals' traits at the micro level, drawing from psychology, economics, and behavioral science (Becker, 1964; Lepak & Snell, 1999; Spearman, 1927). The focus of this approach rested on individuals' personal traits (i.e., KSAOs) and how to drive these traits for motivational and incentive purposes.

However, this approach too suffered from several ambiguities and inconsistencies, especially concerning the so-called "more is better" approach, which neglects a non-additivity issue affecting resources at the unit level (Vassolo, Anand, & Folta, 2004) and the unwillingness of human capital to make their skills, expertise, and abilities firm-specific knowledge and, as such, less valued upon moving to a different firm/context (Raffiee & Coff, 2016). In addition, the micro-level approach overlooked that individual-level human capital must be transformed into unit/firm-level resources by means of appropriate processes at the organizational level (Ployhart & Moliterno, 2011). With respect to the "more is better" fallacy, the non-additivity of human capital is evident if we take account of complementarity among organizational roles, with respect to experience, motivation, and career lifecycle (Berman et al., 2002; Lepak & Snell, 1999). In the context of team-based tasks, in particular, it is important to match domain expertise and field experience appropriately (Taylor & Greve, 2006). When deploying human capital for a given task, therefore, it should be considered whether the selected individuals match correctly and how their contribution to the overall team performance satisfies the additivity requirement, since a given human capital's effort may provide different value contributions under different conditions of utilization/deployment (for a detailed examination of how human capital contribution is likely to differ under heterogeneous contingencies, see Campbell, Coff, & Kryscynski, 2012; Coff, 1997).

Another critical assumption in the context of the micro-level approach concerns an individual's orientation and personal judgment with regard to their alignment with a unit's goals and strategy by means of dedicated and firm-specific on-the-job training and/or other educational activities, since this sort of alignment will transform an individual's generic human capital into firm-specific knowledge. Because individuals may fear that either their future employment opportunities are likely to decrease if their skills are deemed firm specific or that they are likely to be tied to the company under unfavorable conditions if employers are going to act opportunistically once investment in firm-specific skills have been made by employees, it is likely that they will not invest adequately in firm-specific training programs.

Finally, another major critical issue in the context of micro-level studies concerns the way collective, higher-order human capital resources emerge from available KSAOs held at the individual level. Although Ployhart and Moliterno (2011) tried to clarify in detail the multilevel emergent process by means of which individuals' KSAOs evolve into organizational higher-order human capital, this approach falls short of providing a detailed examination of the multilevel interaction between the micro level (i.e., KSAOs at the individual level) and the meso level (i.e., middle management KSAOs and decision making) and how this may reverberate at the macro level, that is, at the overall corporate strategic decision-making level.

To combat the conceptual and methodological fallacies so far highlighted, we maintain that a detailed multilevel approach to human capital must include the meso-managerial level and consider the interaction between the macro and the meso levels, as well as between the meso and the micro levels. More precisely, we maintain that a thorough and consistent understanding of how individual KSAOs evolve into unit/firm-level higher-order resources should include the following issues:

* A detailed examination of the top management/ownership's goals with respect to human capital acquisition, renovation, integration, and development. This is an almost completely neglected theme in the context of strategic management studies, but overlooking this issue is a major misjudgment since individual KSAOs are not constant throughout the work life of individuals, nor do they have the same

value and relevance throughout an individual's job life (Campbell et al., 2012).

- A fine-grained understanding of the role played by managers at the meso level and a detailed understanding of their motivation, taking into account their present career ambitions and future opportunities either with the current employer or with other companies. Both conditions (that is, present ambitions and future opportunities) will likely influence meso-level decisions regarding human capital's utilization of KSAOs at the unit level. Therefore, their deployment will be contingent on the convergence between macro-managerial goals and meso-managerial present and future benefit evaluations.

- A deeper examination of human capital characteristics in order to investigate whether, besides firm-specificity considerations à la Campbell et al. (2012), other relevant issues must be considered when introducing recurrently new human capital resources into established organizational processes for human capital renovation purposes. Indeed, it must be considered that human capital is neither a monolith nor a fixed stock, but that it constitutes a dynamic endowment subject to integration, obsolescence, non-additivity, complementarity, and scale contingencies.

In the following sections we address these aspects in detail and introduce a conceptual framework along with a managerial model for the development of a thorough and consistent strategic human capital approach.

4.2   GETTING STARTED ON SHC MANAGEMENT

Campbell et al. (2012) clarified that human capital value for a given organization is contingent on both demand- and supply-side considerations and conditions. Taking account of this important premise, and assuming that firms will meet the required criteria regarding individuals' KSAOs acquisition, it is not a given that, despite individuals' willingness to adhere to their organization's goals, human capital integration and development will be carried out following top management/ownership strategy. More precisely, it is important to recall that this strategy must be consistently implemented by middle managers at the meso-organizational level. Therefore, the top management/ownership's goals should be considered and also why they might be hindered by a non-aligned orientation and/or conduct at the meso level.

First, because human capital is not a fixed stock but a multifaceted and dynamic endowment, a firm's top management/ownership must progress towards its renewal recurrently following a planned approach and avoid incurring emergent and non-planned decisions, unless these are depending on employees' autonomous decision to leave the company. This implies that corporate-level decision making with respect to human capital resources acquisition must take account of how they will be, in turn, integrated and developed at the unit/firm level. Indeed, it does not suffice to acquire human capital resources to automatically integrate and develop them within established organizational processes, since these resources, once recruited and acquired, must be allocated to a specific division/function and subsequently must actually be deployed at the unit level to carry out the task for which they have been recruited. Because human capital constitutes a dynamic resource endowment, the top management/ownership level must plan and organize a continuous renewal program in the context of human resources and related KSAOs for at least two fundamental reasons: (1) newcomers' integration requires time and suffers from time compression,[1] thus this activity must be carried out within an appropriate period of time; (2) human capital development creates a unit's shared experience, which, in turn, is highly context specific, that is, once the individuals sharing a given experience are replaced or leave the unit, the shared experience must be reconstructed among the newcomers and remaining individuals. Therefore, it is of the utmost importance that newcomers and existing unit members interact and work together adequately, otherwise newcomers' integration and development will not be achieved.

Second, despite the inherent value of a newly recruited individual, extant literature theoretically maintained and empirically observed that newcomers often do not contribute positively to the unit's performance in the short term due to a lack of tacit knowledge, languages, schemata, and other context-specific aspects of competence that can be acquired only over time and by means of continuous involvement and integration in the unit's tasks and processes. Because newcomers' deployment, integration, and development are the responsibility of those at a meso-managerial level also responsible for unit performance, the latter are not inclined to trade poor short-term performance at the unit level for long-term success, mostly as they may be removed from their position because of this poor short-term performance and, thus, will not partake in this long-term success. Thus, it is likely that newcomers will not be deployed to the extent required by top management/ownership. However, top management/ownership will not be able to ascertain whether newly acquired human capital are being integrated and developed to the desired extent, which gives rise to a critical agency problem (Eisenhardt, 1989). More precisely, managers at the meso level, who are in charge of newly acquired human capital, represent an important element in the execution of a given strategy, since they are in between the macro top management/ownership level and the micro-operations level. In addition, different from other human capital, managers at the meso level are characterized by more frequent mobility, thus they are more sensitive to short-term results as compared to other human capital resources located at the micro level in the context of organizational activities. The higher mobility of managers at the meso level emphasizes the importance to them of short-term results, since their success will rest, mostly, on this type of performance. A high level of performance of the unit they lead, indeed, will foster their reputation and increase both the chance to obtain either rewards from the current employer or new offers from a different employer, whereas, instead, poor short-term performance will jeopardize their tenure at the current employer and reduce the opportunity to obtain new job offers from other employers. In sum, if the meso-managerial level is not adequately involved in the long-term strategy, it is likely that new human capital integration will not be carried out adequately and the overall corporate human capital strategy will be hindered.

Third, human capital acquisition should focus on a fine-grained examination of KSAOs and how these important characteristics interact with the meso-managerial level. This is a quite overlooked and under-investigated area of study, since organizations compete fiercely for high-quality human capital and talent and try to acquire them in order to achieve high-quality performance. However, Cattani, Ferriani, Mariani, and Mengoli (2013) observed, in the context of Hollywood film-making, that star-studded projects do not always lead to adequate performance and that instead team familiarity and previous interactions among team members reduce conflict and enhance performance. Likewise, it has been observed in the financial investments industry that assembling too many high-status employees does not bring the expected results and that "too many cooks spoil the broth" (Groysberg, Polzer, & Elfenbein, 2011). In essence, besides competing for talented human capital and creating star-studded teams, top managers and owners should also focus on KSAOs' heterogeneity and how it should affect newly acquired human capital integration and interaction with both existing teammates and managers at the meso level. Therefore, an effective human capital development strategy should pay attention to interaction and integration dynamics at the unit level, moving beyond the traditional motivation and incentive activities.

In the next section we introduce a conceptual model for strategic human capital management that addresses the above issues.

4.3   A MODEL FOR SHC MANAGEMENT: GOALS, DIMENSIONS, AND RESULTS

In this section we provide a conceptual model of the development of strategic human capital resources at the unit/firm level. On the basis of the theoretical advances and empirical evidence reported in previous chapters, we assume that an organization's future competitiveness rests on the effective and continuous integration of new human resources and on the alignment between the macro and the meso levels with respect to human capital integration and development.

In particular, our model offers a 2×2 matrix in the context of which the macro and the meso levels, that is, the top management/owner in charge of human capital strategy and the middle manager responsible for its execution act as the principal and the agent, respectively, of an agency-based model. Accordingly, the model's cells identify two main orientations as regards both principal and agent, namely, short term and long term. Therefore, our 2×2 model includes four cells (Figure 4.2):

1. principal (short term)–agent (short term);
2. principal (long term)–agent (short term);
3. principal (short term)–agent (long term);
4. principal (long term)–agent (long term).

This model enables the identification of four different scenarios of human capital renewal, assuming that this renewal is a fundamental antecedent of new competence development at the whole organizational level, and this, however, can be achieved only if the agent implements the principal's human capital strategy correctly.

By means of this model, we provide a fine-grained understanding with respect to the potential conflict between different managerial levels and the related implication of the agency costs concerning new knowledge and competences developed at the organizational level. Finally, the conceptual framework advanced by our model allows us to identify an appropriate strategy to overcome the potential misalignment and

Long term	New knowledge development vs reputation	New knowledge development and future opportunity in the organization
Top manager/owner *Principal*		
	Integration vs reputation	Integration without middle management engagement vs future opportunity in other firms
Short term		

Short term   Middle manager   Long term

Agent

Figure 4.2   Agency problems in the context of the renewal of human capital resources

conflict between principal and agent. Figure 4.2 shows our conceptual framework.

Before examining the content of each cell in Figure 4.2, we provide a brief summary of the principal's and the agent's respective goals and expectations. From the principal's viewpoint, human resource renewal decisions require appropriate planning at the corporate level because human capital renewal enables new knowledge development, which in turn sustains an organization's innovation processes and thus helps reduce predictability and knowledge ossification. By periodically replacing outgoing people with newcomers though, a given organization suffers from a continuous loss in terms of shared experience and collective tacit knowledge, an occurrence that leads to poor short-term performance, as we have empirically demonstrated in Chapter 3. A poor short-term performance at the team/unit level in turn represents a major concern for the agent, since they are valued mostly with respect to their ability to lead their team over a short-term time frame. Therefore, although newcomers' integration at the unit/team level is a fundamental step in the principal's strategy, its actual execution constitutes a source of conflict and ambiguity at the team/unit level. In particular, poor short-term results are likely to negatively affect an agent's reputation and career because they reduce both the chance that the agent will continue his collaboration

Table 4.1   *Prisoner's dilemma pay-off explanation*

Pay-off	Explanation
4	It is the highest pay-off; however, it cannot be achieved by both players simultaneously, but only by one player at the expense of the other
3	It is the second-highest pay-off; it can be achieved by both players simultaneously, but only if they adopt a cooperative and long-term orientation
2	It is the third-highest pay-off; it is achieved by both players simultaneously when they act on the basis of mutual distrust and short-term orientation
1	It is the lowest pay-off; it is achieved by one of the players when the other one acts opportunistically and maximizes his short-term results

with the current employer and their future career opportunities at other organizations.

Therefore, the principal must navigate through several contingencies to achieve an effective human capital strategy that obtains both newcomers' integration and development and the agent's cooperation. To address these contingencies by means of a thorough conceptual framework, we adopt a "prisoner's dilemma" approach to investigate how the principal and the agent act in the context of human capital renewal decisions. We adopt a game-theory approach to emphasize the dynamic interaction that occurs between the two managerial levels considered, and also to highlight that two rational actors may have difficulty fully cooperating although they have, apparently, a common interest and should pursue a common goal. Figure 4.2 displays our model, while Table 4.1 reports the pay-off rank. To allow for a stylized representation, we assume four possible pay-offs, as follows in Table 4.1:

- *Principal short/agent short.* In this cell we observe an occurrence based on mutual distrust with regard to the level of deployment of newly acquired assets. In particular, the principal (P) will not achieve his goal in terms of new assets utilization and integration because the agent (A) is concerned that a major involvement of these new resources will engender a negative performance, therefore he will resist P's request regarding the integration of these new assets. As a result, a satisficing level of human capital development will not be achieved, which, in turn will hamper both human capital strategy and macro-level–meso-level cooperation. In this case, both P and A receive a low pay-off, since they will not be able to pursue their goals. Pay-off combination: 2,2.

- *Principal long/agent short.* In this cell, A will resist P's request for new assets' integration, thus his short-term orientation will result in a minimum if not null deployment of new employees, and, given that P is interested in the long-term strategy implementation of his plan, it is likely that he will not be preoccupied with short-term results (similarly to "The Process" of the Philadelphia 76ers; see Preface). A short-term orientation of A implies instead that he will be preoccupied with high-quality short-term results with the current organization, on which to build his future career and employment opportunities, either with the current or with other employers. Therefore, to maximize his future career opportunities he will not involve the new assets, whose integration is likely to contribute negatively to the unit's short-term results. Therefore, P will achieve the lowest pay-off, whereas instead A will maximize his result at the expense of P's human capital strategy. Pay-off combination: 1,4.
- *Principal short/agent long.* In this cell, P requires that A deploys the new asset to a major extent and adopts tight monitoring to check whether this integration is carried out to the required degree. Because A understands this requirement as an opportunity to achieve a long-lasting tenure with the current employer, it is likely that he will deploy newcomers to a significant degree, notwithstanding that the potential poor short-term results will harm his reputation and future employment opportunities with other potential employers. Therefore, A is inclined to execute P's strategy with regard to new resources' integration. In this case, it is likely that the new assets will be integrated in the unit's short-term operations and that this occurrence will bring about a negative performance. As a result, P's strategy in terms of new human capital integration will be achieved at the expense of A's reputation and other opportunities in terms of future jobs and career development, if the given unit performs poorly for a prolonged period of time. Pay-off combination: 4,1.
- *Principal long/agent long.* In this case, both P and A adopt a long-term orientation. Therefore, the former is not concerned whether the latter does not deploy the new asset to a major extent, insofar as A will, however, be supportive of the long-term strategy of P. By the same token, A will not be concerned with P's long-term orientation, because he will not be tightly monitored, and this will allow him to reach an acceptable level of integration of the newly acquired human resources. In this case, both P and A will achieve a satisficing outcome, since to implement a long-term strategy they both need to

mutually accept each other's requirements. This means that newly acquired human resources can be integrated to an acceptable extent and that this should not happen at A's expense, whose reputation in case of short-term poor performance must be supported and the unit's poor performance should not result in his removal. In this case, both P and A will be able to achieve their long-term goals and, in turn, a relatively high outcome. Pay-off combination: 3,3.

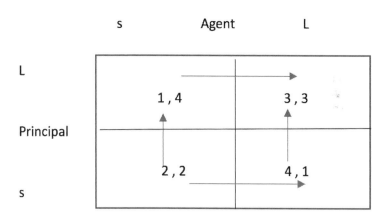

Figure 4.3   *A prisoner's dilemma approach to human capital development*

The solution to the prisoner's dilemma (Figure 4.3) – assuming that both P and A are rational individuals – leads, however, to a suboptimal combination of pay-offs, that is, that characterized by a short-term orientation of both managerial levels, which leads to the third available pay-off for both players (2,2). This outcome is obtained because, following the arrows in Figure 4.3, the pay-offs associated with short-term results are higher than those associated with long-term results for both the principal and the agent, an occurrence that leads to the identification of a dominant strategy for both players, that is, a situation in which neither of the two players have reason or incentive to change their behavior (i.e., a situation known as a Nash equilibrium). However, because human capital development requires a long-term orientation, they could both achieve a higher pay-off (3,3) if they opt for a cooperative stance. But, to reach an effective cooperation and alignment, a risk-sharing policy must be adopted. To this end, several appropriate human capital management tools should be adopted. In the remainder of this section we briefly introduce these tools:

1. *Performance management systems.* The implementation of any rewards program, whose purpose is to align different managerial levels' interests, requires the definition of a model of performance management, since the decisions regarding employees' careers are based on performance evaluations. However, when human capital activities are not easy to assess, the definition of an effective performance management system is a quite difficult organizational task. In order to develop and implement a satisficing performance management process, first a set of performance dimensions should be identified with respect to both middle managers' and newcomers' roles and duties. Because top management/ownership goals entail both their unit performance and human capital integration, an accurate performance management system will help clarify what the top management/ownership expectations are and how potential conflicts and misunderstandings can be solved before they jeopardize a unit's/firm's competitiveness.

2. *Recognition programs.* Because a poor cooperative attitude and a short-term orientation may damage a unit's performance and survival, in the short run a recognition program should be implemented to support individuals' reputations. Different from incentives, whose goal is to obtain a change in an individual's behavior, a recognition program aims to recognize behaviors that follow specific values and orientation, which, given their intrinsic nature, are quite difficult to define and observe. With respect to human capital integration and development, an adequate integration of newcomers is difficult to assess because it is difficult to define exactly what conduct a middle manager should adopt, and therefore how to provide support to a given renewal strategy (Herzberg, 1968; Maslow, 1970). According to Rath and Clifton (2004) recognition programs increase employees' productivity, their engagement among peers, and retention rate. Since recognition is all about message rather than reward, it is a highly effective tool when performance is either decreasing or inadequate. However, to be truly effective, a recognition program must be carefully planned, especially with respect to the dimensions upon which the alignment between different managerial goals must be achieved.

3. *Bonuses.* A bonus is a specific reward, to be bestowed once a given task has been successfully carried out following specific prescriptions

and instructions. One of the main types of bonus that could reduce a misalignment in the short-term goals between the principal (top management) and the agent (middle management) is the project bonus. In particular, when newcomers join a team/unit, a project bonus for a middle manager may be linked to the successful integration of these individuals.

4. *Long-term relational contracts.* A long-term relational contract is a particular type of agreement between two individuals who act at different managerial levels and have a shared interest in obtaining a fruitful compromise that promotes an effective long-term cooperation. Studies in the context of leader–member exchange theory (LMX: Foa & Foa, 1974; Wilson, Sin, & Conlon, 2010) observed that by means of the LMX approach, different goals can be simultaneously achieved, since it allows for a clear examination and appraisal of both leaders' and members' expectations and goals. By means of a long-term relational contract, therefore, the principal and the agent agree on a set of benefits, some of which are very concrete (money, gifts), while others are quite abstract (status, service, information). The important contribution of this approach is that an owner/top manager and a middle manager may cooperate and agree on a specific set of heterogeneous resources, thus achieving their respective goals without putting at risk the team's/unit's long-term viability and survival.

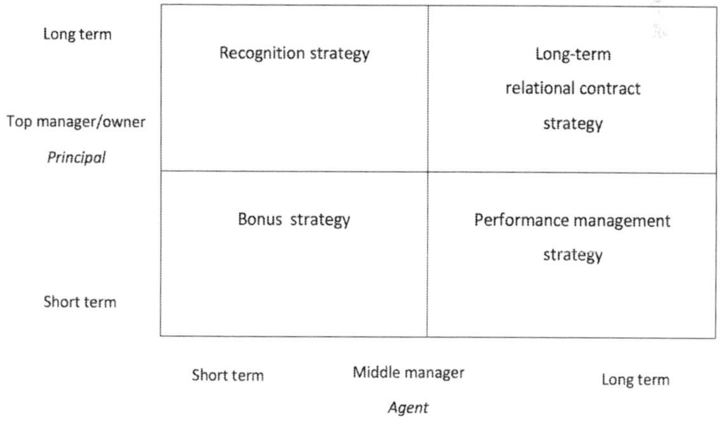

	Short term (Middle manager / Agent)	Long term (Middle manager / Agent)
Long term (Top manager/owner / Principal)	Recognition strategy	Long-term relational contract strategy
Short term	Bonus strategy	Performance management strategy

Figure 4.4   *Solving agency problems in the context of the renewal of human capital resources*

Figure 4.4 summarizes the above approaches to the solution of macro-level–meso-level conflict.

4.4   CONCLUSION: MONITORING SHC ADEQUACY AND PREVENTING RIGIDITIES AND OBSOLESCENCE

Throughout this book we have suggested a number of conceptual advances supported by the empirical evidence reported in Chapters 2 and 3, as well as by the theoretical framework illustrated above. In particular, we have successfully addressed the challenges highlighted in the first chapter of this book, since our empirical evidence has clarified several important ambiguities and provided important conceptual insights. In particular, in Chapter 2, we have clarified that the actual relationship between shared experience and organizations' results, empirically observed by means of our quasi-replication, is non-monotonic. More precisely, we clarified that the hypothesized inverted-U shaped relationship, although empirically supported by means of our analyses, in fact, once examined through the actual distribution of our observations, was actually an increasing relationship, yet at a decreasing rate. Furthermore, we found support for this relationship when we articulated our analysis with respect to the different organizational roles examined (i.e., routinized vs creative), while instead the same analysis carried out at the whole organizational level reported a non-significant result. This is a very important clarification with respect to the ambiguity of previous results in the context of the relationship between shared experience and performance, since we tackled the major ambiguity that maintained either a linear or an inverted-U shaped relationship. We found, instead, a relationship that increases at a decreasing rate, specifically with respect to both creative and routinized roles, which suggests that the advantages of shared experience must be managed by means of human capital renewal, in the context of specific organizational roles.

We provided further conceptual advances by examining how human capital renewal is actually carried out and what its effects are. More precisely, in Chapter 3, we investigated whether specific decisions in the context of the human capital strategy affected organizational results, and how. In particular, we clarified that releasing co-specialized human capital affects performance negatively and that therefore it should be carried out at an appropriate pace and with a balanced approach. Furthermore, we found that general expertise at the industry level, when brought into a given organization, has no significant effect on performance, while, instead, not paying adequate attention to newcomers' expertise heterogeneity negatively affects a unit's results. Finally, we also found that negative organizational performance may result in middle manager replacement, thus providing empirical support for the potential conflict/ambiguity between different managerial levels interested in human capital renewal.

In summary, our results provided a pronounced array of evidence with regard to the advancement of a human capital strategy that aims to encompass the macro, the meso, and the micro levels. In a parallel fashion, the above evidence provides a notable set of contributions, since our overarching research goal was to determine how an effective human capital strategy should be crafted, taking account of:

- the different managerial levels involved in this highly relevant activity, namely, the macro and the meso levels, and the potential conflict and misalignment between these two levels;
- the need to proceed, periodically, to human capital endowment renewal, to reduce organizational inertia, ossification, and predictability; and
- the inherent problems associated with human capital renewal, in terms of loss of shared experience of outgoing human capital and the uncertain contribution to performance of newcomers.

Because human capital is one of the most important of all organizational resources, and given that its development is influenced by several intervening phenomena, we maintain that one of the most relevant and critical activities involves the prevention of SHC obsolescence, ossification, and inadequacy to the various contingencies of contemporary business landscape. To fulfill this aim, we advanced a multilevel SHC model that encompasses the fundamental role of a firm's top management/ ownership with respect to human capital strategy formulation, the often overlooked role of managers at the meso level of human capital integration and development, and finally, the analysis of KSAOs in terms of heterogeneity with respect to existing human resources and as a whole human capital bundle. However, we did not restrict our analysis to the mere descriptive stage with respect to the existence of these three levels, since we also predicted a series of consequences with respect to the different orientations observed at the various levels of observation (i.e., macro, meso and micro), and, finally, we offered specific prescriptions and a novel conceptual framework with respect to SHC management.

Our purpose was to fill the gaps and address the several inconsistencies and ambiguities originating from the lack of conversation between strategic management and human resource management, and to open up a dialogue between these two quite separate theoretical domains. We are confident that this book has realized its goals and that our insights will help the investigation of new research avenues as well as help to achieve renewed managerial effectiveness in the context of SHC management.

NOTE

1. A widely used expression in management literature that means that you cannot accelerate a given process's execution, because it takes a given amount of time and doing it in a shorter time period is not useful.

References

Ackerman, P. L., & Heggestad, E. D. (1997). Intelligence, personality, and interests: Evidence for overlapping traits. *Psychological Bulletin, 121*(2), 219–245.

Almanacco Illustrato del Calcio [Illustrated yearbook of Italian football] (various years). Modena: Franco Cosimo Panini.

Amit, R., & Schoemaker, P. J. (1993). Strategic assets and organizational rent. *Strategic Management Journal, 14*(1), 33–46.

Argote, L. (1999). *Organizational learning: Creating, retaining, and transferring knowledge*. Boston, MA: Kluwer Academic.

Argote, L., Devadas, R., & Melone, N. (1990). The base-rate fallacy: Contrasting processes and outcomes of group and individual judgment. *Organizational Behavior and Human Decision Processes, 46*(2), 296–310.

Audia, P. G., & Greve, H. R. (2006). Less likely to fail: Low performance, firm size, and factory expansion in the shipbuilding industry. *Management Science, 52*(1), 83–94.

Barney, J. B. (1986). Strategic factor markets: Expectations, luck, and business strategy. *Management Science, 32*(10), 1231–1241.

Barney, J. B. (1991). Firm resources and sustained competitive advantage. *Journal of Management, 17*(1), 99–120.

Barney, J. B., & Felin, T. (2013). What are microfoundations? *Academy of Management Perspectives, 27*, 138–155.

Barney, J. B., & Wright, P. M. (1998). On becoming a strategic partner: The role of human resources in gaining competitive advantage. *Human Resource Management, 37*(1), 31–46.

Bauer, T. N., Morrison, E. W., & Callister, R. R. (1998). Organizational socialization research: A review and directions for future research. *Research in Personnel and Human Resources Management, 16*, 149–214.

Baum, J. A. C., & Ingram, P. (1998). Survival-enhancing learning in the Manhattan hotel industry, 1898–1980. *Management Science, 44*(7), 996–1016.

Becker, B., & Gerhart, B. (1996). The impact of human resource management on organizational performance: Progress and prospects. *Academy of Management Journal, 39*(4), 779–801.

Becker, G. S. (1964). *Human capital theory*. New York: Columbia University Press.

Becker, G. S. (2002). The age of human capital. In E. P. Lazear (Ed.), *Education in the twenty-first century* (pp. 3–8). Palo Alto, CA: Hoover Institution Press.

Bergh, D. D. (1995). Size and relatedness of units sold: An agency theory and resource-based perspective. *Strategic Management Journal, 16*(3), 221–239.

Berle, A. A., & Means, G. C. (1932). *The modern corporation and private property*. New York: Macmillan.

Berman, S. L., Down, J., & Hill, C. W. L. (2002). Tacit knowledge as a source of competitive advantage in the National Basketball Association. *Academy of Management Journal*, *45*(1), 13–31.

Bettis, R. A., Helfat, C. E., & Shaver, J. M. (2016). The necessity, logic, and forms of replication. *Strategic Management Journal*, *37*, 2193–2203.

Bowen, H. P., & Wiersema, M. F. (1999). Matching method to paradigm in strategy research: Limitations of cross-sectional analysis and some methodological alternatives. *Strategic Management Journal*, *20*(7), 625–636.

Brera, G. (1975). *Storia critica del calcio italiano* [Critical history of Italian football]. Milan: Bompiani.

Brymer, R. A., Molloy, J. C., & Gilbert, B. A. (2014). Human capital pipelines: Competitive implications of repeated interorganizational hiring. *Journal of Management*, *40*(2), 483–508.

Campbell, B. A., Coff, R., & Kryscynski, D. (2012). Rethinking sustained competitive advantage from human capital. *Academy of Management Review*, *37*(3), 376–395.

Campbell, B. A., Saxton, B. M., & Banerjee, P. M. (2014). Resetting the shot clock: The effect of comobility on human capital. *Journal of Management*, *40*(2), 531–556.

Carpenter, M. A., Sanders, W. G., & Gregersen, H. B. (2001). Bundling human capital with organizational context: The impact of international assignment experience on multinational firm performance and CEO pay. *Academy of Management Journal*, *44*(3), 493–511.

Carroll, G. R. (1993). A sociological view on why firms differ. *Strategic Management Journal*, *14*(4), 237–249.

Castanias, R. P., & Helfat, C. E. (1991). Managerial resources and rents. *Journal of Management*, *17*(1), 155–171.

Cattani, G., Ferriani, S., Mariani, M. M., & Mengoli, S. (2013). Tackling the "Galàcticos" effect: Team familiarity and the performance of star-studded projects. *Industrial and Corporate Change*, *22*(6), 1629–1662.

Chatterjee, S., Hadi, A. S., & Price, B. (2000). *Regression analysis by example.* Hoboken, NJ: John Wiley & Sons.

Chen, G. (2005). Newcomer adaptation in teams: Multilevel antecedents and outcomes. *Academy of Management Journal*, *48*(1), 101–116.

Chen, G., & Klimoski, R. J. (2003). The impact of expectations on newcomer performance in teams as mediated by work characteristics, social exchanges, and empowerment. *Academy of Management Journal*, *46*(5), 591–607.

Coff, R. W. (1997). Human assets and management dilemmas: Coping with hazards on the road to resource-based theory. *Academy of Management Review*, *22*(2), 374–402.

Coff, R. W. (1999). When competitive advantage doesn't lead to performance: The resource-based view and stakeholder bargaining power. *Organization Science*, *10*(2), 119–133.

Coff, R., & Kryscynski, D. (2011). Invited editorial: Drilling for micro-foundations of human capital-based competitive advantages. *Journal of Management*, *37*, 1429–1443.

Cohen, W. M., & Levinthal, D. A. (1990). Absorptive capacity: A new perspective on learning and innovation. *Administrative Science Quarterly, 35*(1), 128–152.

Combs, J., Liu, Y., Hall, A., & Ketchen, D. (2006). How much do high-performance work practices matter? A meta-analysis of their effects on organizational performance. *Personnel Psychology, 59*(3), 501–528.

Cool, K., Dierickx, I., & Jemison, D. (1989). Business strategy, market structure and risk–return relationships: A structural approach. *Strategic Management Journal, 10*(6), 507–522.

Crocker, A., & Eckardt, R. (2014). A multilevel investigation of individual- and unit-level human capital complementarities. *Journal of Management, 40*(2), 509–530.

Crook, T. R., Todd, S. Y., Combs, J. G., Woehr, D. J., & Ketchen Jr., D. J. (2011). Does human capital matter? A meta-analysis of the relationship between human capital and firm performance. *Journal of Applied Psychology, 96*(3), 443–456.

Dalton, D., Hitt, M., Certo, S. T., & Dalton, C. (2007). The fundamental agency problem and its mitigation: Independence, equity, and the market for corporate control. *The Academy of Management Annals, 1*(1), 1–64.

Day, D. V., Gordon, S., & Fink, C. (2012). The sporting life: Exploring organizations through the lens of sport. *The Academy of Management Annals, 6*(1), 397–433.

Dirks, K. T. (2000). Trust in leadership and team performance: Evidence from NCAA basketball. *Journal of Applied Psychology, 85*(6), 1004–1112.

Dokko, G., Wilk, S. L., & Rothbard, N. P. (2009). Unpacking prior experience: How career history affects job performance. *Organization Science, 20*(1), 51–68.

Edmondson, A. C., Bohmer, R. M., & Pisano, G. P. (2001). Disrupted routines: Team learning and new technology implementation in hospitals. *Administrative Science Quarterly, 46*(4), 685–716.

Eisenhardt, K. M. (1989). Agency theory: An assessment and review. *The Academy of Management Review, 14*(1), 57–74.

Eisenhardt, K. M., & Martin, J. A. (2000). Dynamic capabilities: What are they? *Strategic Management Journal, 21*(10–11), 1105–1121.

Enciclopedia Panini del Calcio Italiano, 1960–2000 [Panini encyclopedia of Italian football, 1960–2000] (2000). Modena: Franco Cosimo Panini.

Fama, E. F., & Jensen, M. C. (1983). Separation of ownership and control. *Journal of Law and Economics, 26*(2), 301–325.

Foa, U. G., & Foa, E. B. (1974). *Societal structures of the mind.* Springfield, IL: Charles C. Thomas.

Foot, J. (2007). *A history of Italian football.* London: Harper Perennial.

Fulmer, I. S., & Ployhart, R. E. (2014). "Our most important asset": A multidisciplinary/multilevel review of human capital valuation for research and practice. *Journal of Management, 40*(1), 161–192.

Gilbert, C. G. (2005). Unbundling the structure of inertia: Resource versus routine rigidity. *Academy of Management Journal, 48*(5), 741–763.

Gottfredson, L. S. (1997). Why g matters: The complexity of everyday life. *Intelligence*, *24*(1), 79–132.

Grant, R. M. (1996). Toward a knowledge-based theory of the firm. *Strategic Management Journal*, *17*, 109–122.

Greene, W. W. H. (2003). *Econometric analysis*. Upper Saddle River, NJ: Prentice Hall.

Greve, H. R. (2003). A behavioral theory of R&D expenditures and innovations: Evidence from shipbuilding. *Academy of Management Journal*, *46*(6), 685–702.

Grigoriou, K., & Rothaermel, F. T. (2014). Structural microfoundations of innovation: The role of relational stars. *Journal of Management*, *40*(2), 586–615.

Groysberg, B., & Lee, L. E. (2009). Hiring stars and their colleagues: Exploration and exploitation in professional service firms. *Organization Science*, *20*(4), 740–758.

Groysberg, B., Lee, L. E., & Nanda, A. (2008). Can they take it with them? The portability of star knowledge workers' performance. *Management Science*, *54*(7), 1213–1230.

Groysberg, B., Polzer, J. T., & Elfenbein, H. A. (2011). Too many cooks spoil the broth: How high-status individuals decrease group effectiveness. *Organization Science*, *22*(3), 722–737.

Guion, R. M. (2011). *Assessment, measurement, and prediction for personnel decisions* (2nd ed.). New York: Routledge.

Hambrick, D. C., Cho, T. S., & Chen, M. J. (1996). The influence of top management team heterogeneity on firms' competitive moves. *Administrative Science Quarterly*, *41*(4), 659–684.

Hatch, N. W., & Dyer, J. H. (2004). Human capital and learning as a source of sustainable competitive advantage. *Strategic Management Journal*, *25*(12), 1155–1178.

Herzberg, F. (1968). One more time: How do you motivate employees? *Harvard Business Review*, *46*(1), 53–62.

Hess, A. M., & Rothaermel, F. T. (2011). When are assets complementary? Star scientists, strategic alliances, and innovation in the pharmaceutical industry. *Strategic Management Journal*, *32*(8), 895–909.

Hitt, M. A., Biermant, L., Shimizu, K., & Kochhar, R. (2001). Direct and moderating effects of human capital on strategy and performance in professional service firms: A resource-based perspective. *Academy of Management Journal*, *44*(1), 13–28.

Holcomb, T. R., Holmes, R. M., & Connelly, B. L. (2009). Making the most of what you have: Managerial ability as a source of resource value creation. *Strategic Management Journal*, *30*(5), 457–485.

Holland, J. R. (1997). *Making vacational choice: A theory of vacational personalities*. Odessa, FL: PAR.

Huckman, R. S., & Pisano, G. P. (2006). The firm specificity of individual performance: Evidence from cardiac surgery. *Management Science*, *52*(4), 473–488.

Huckman, R. S., Staats, B. R., & Upton, D. M. (2009). Team familiarity, role experience, and performance: Evidence from Indian software services. *IEEE Engineering Management Review*, *40*(1), 99–118.

Huselid, M. A. (1995). The impact of human resource management practices on turnover, productivity, and corporate financial performance. *Academy of Management Journal, 38*(3), 635–672.

Huselid, M. A., Jackson, S. E., & Schuler, R. S. (1997). Technical and strategic human resources management effectiveness as determinants of firm performance. *Academy of Management Journal, 40*(1), 171–188.

Jensen, A. R. (1998). *The g factor: The science of mental ability.* Westport, CT: Greenwood.

Jensen, M. C., & Meckling, W. H. (1976). Theory of the firm: Managerial behavior, agency costs and ownership structure. *Journal of Financial Economics, 3*(4), 305–360.

Kahneman, D., & Tversky, A. (1979). Prospect theory: An analysis of decision under risk. *Econometrica, 47*(2), 263–292.

Kanfer, R. (1990). Motivation and individual differences in learning: An integration of developmental, differential and cognitive perspectives. *Learning and Individual Differences, 2*(2), 221–239.

Katz, R. (1982). The effects of group longevity on project communication and performance. *Administrative Science Quarterly, 27*(1), 81–104.

Khanna, P., Jones, C. D., & Boivie, S. (2014). Director human capital, information processing demands, and board effectiveness. *Journal of Management, 40*(2), 557–585.

Kogut, B., & Zander, U. (1992). Knowledge of the firm, combinative capabilities, and the replication of technology. *Organization Science, 3*(3), 383–397.

Kor, Y. Y., & Leblebici, H. (2005). How do interdependencies among human-capital deployment, development, and diversification strategies affect firms' financial performance? *Strategic Management Journal, 26*(10), 967–985.

Kozlowski, S. W. J., & Klein, K. J. (2000). A multilevel approach to theory and research in organizations: Contextual, temporal, and emergent processes. In K. J. Klein & S. W. J. Kozlowski (Eds.), *Multilevel theory, research and methods in organizations: Foundations, extensions, and new directions* (pp. 3–90). San Francisco, CA: Jossey-Bass.

Leonard-Barton, D. (1995). *Wellsprings of knowledge: Building and sustaining the sources of innovation.* Boston, MA: Harvard Business School Press.

Leonard-Barton, D. (1992 [2011]). Core capabilities and core rigidities: A paradox in managing new product development. In D. A. Leonard, *Managing Knowledge Assets, Creativity and Innovation* (pp. 13–27). Singapore: World Scientific Publishing.

Lepak, D. P., & Gowan, M. (2010). *Human resource management.* Upper Saddle River, NJ: Pearson/Prentice Hall.

Lepak, D. P., & Snell, S. A. (1999). The human resource architecture: Toward a theory of human capital allocation and development. *Academy of Management Review, 24*(1), 31–48.

Levinthal, D. A., & March, J. G. (1993). The myopia of learning. *Strategic Management Journal, 14*(S2), 95–112.

Levitt, B., & March, J. G. (1988). Organizational learning. *Annual Review of Sociology, 14*, 319–340.

Liu, K. (2014). Human capital, social collaboration, and patent renewal within U.S. pharmaceutical firms. *Journal of Management, 40*(2), 616–636.

Liu, X., Van Jaarsveld, D. D., Batt, R., & Frost, A. C. (2014). The influence of capital structure on strategic human capital: Evidence from U.S. and Canadian firms. *Journal of Management, 40*(2), 422–448.

Mackey, A., Molloy, J. C., & Morris, S. S. (2014). Scarce human capital in managerial labor markets. *Journal of Management, 40*(2), 399–421.

Mahoney, J. T. (1995). The management of resources and the resource of management. *Journal of Business Research, 33*(2), 91–101.

Makadok, R. (2001). Toward a synthesis of the resource-based and dynamic-capability views of rent creation. *Strategic Management Journal, 22*(5), 387–401.

March, J. G., & Shapira, Z. (1987). Managerial perspectives on risk and risk taking. *Management Science, 33*(1), 1404–1418.

Maslow, A. H. (1970). *Motivation and personality* (L. Carr, Ed.). New York: Longman.

McCrae, R. R., & Costa, P. T. (1996). Toward a new generation of personality theories: Theoretical contexts for the five-factor model. In J. S. Wiggins (Ed.), *The five-factor model of personality: Theoretical perspectives* (pp. 51–87). New York: Guilford Press.

Moliterno, T. P., & Wiersema, M. F. (2007). Firm performance, rent appropriation, and the strategic resource divestment capability. *Strategic Management Journal, 28*(11), 1065–1087.

Nahapiet, J., & Ghoshal, S. (1998). Social capital, intellectual capital, and the organizational advantage. *Academy of Management Review, 23*(2), 242–266.

Nelson, R., & Winter, S. G. (1982). The Schumpeterian tradeoff revisited. *American Economic Review, 72*(1), 114–132.

Nonaka, I., & Takeuchi, H. (1995). *The knowledge-creating company: How Japanese companies create the dynamics of innovation.* Oxford: Oxford University Press.

Nyberg, A., Fulmer, I., Gerhart, B., & Carpenter, M. (2010). Agency theory revisited: CEO return and shareholder interest alignment. *Academy of Management Journal, 53*(5), 1029–1049.

Nyberg, A. J., Moliterno, T. P., Hale, D., & Lepak, D. P. (2014). Resource based perspectives on unit-level human capital: A review and integration. *Journal of Management, 40*(1), 316–346.

Palacios-Huerta, I. (2016). *Beautiful game theory: How soccer can help economics.* Princeton, NJ: Princeton University Press.

Penrose, E. T. (1959). *The theory of the growth of the firm.* New York: John Wiley & Sons Inc.

Peteraf, M. A. (1993). The cornerstones of competitive advantage: A resource-based view. *Strategic Management Journal, 14*(3), 179–191.

Peteraf, M. A., & Maritan, C. (2007). Dynamic capabilities and organizational process. In C. E. Helfat, S. Finkelstein, W. Mitchell, M. Peteraf, H. Singh, D. J. Teece, & S. G. Winter (Eds), *Dynamic capabilities: Understanding strategic change in organizations* (pp. 30–45). Malden, MA: Blackwell.

Peteraf, M. A., Di Stefano, G., & Verona, G. (2013). The elephant in the room of dynamic capabilities: Bringing two diverging conversations together. *Strategic Management Journal, 34*(12), 1389–1410.

Pfeffer, J., & Davis-Blake, A. (1986). Administrative succession and organizational performance: How administrator experience mediates the succession effect. *Academy of Management Journal, 29*(1), 72–83.

Ployhart, R. E., & Hendricks, J. L. (2019). The missing levels of microfoundations: A call for bottom-up theory and methods. In S. E. Humphrey & J. M. LeBreton (Eds.), *The handbook of multilevel theory, measurement, and analysis* (pp. 141–162). Washington, DC: APA.

Ployhart, R. E., & Moliterno, T. (2011). Emergence of the human capital resource: A multilevel model. *Academy of Management Review, 36*(1), 127–150.

Ployhart, R. E., Nyberg, A. J., Reilly, G., & Maltarich, M. A. (2014). Human capital is dead; long live human capital resources! *Journal of Management, 40*(2), 371–398.

Prahalad, C. K., & Hamel, G. (1990 [2007]). The core competence of the corporation. In D. J. Reifer (Ed.), *Software management* (7th ed.) (pp. 259–271). Chichester: John Wiley & Sons.

Priem, R. L., & Butler, J. E. (2001). Is the resource-based "view" a useful perspective for strategic management research? *Academy of Management Review, 26*(1), 22–40.

Quelch, J., Nueno, J. L., & Knoop, C. I. (2004). Real Madrid Club de Futbol. *Harvard Business School Case Collection*, April.

Quiñones, M. A., Ford, J. K., & Teachout, M. S. (1995). The relationship between work experience and job performance: A conceptual and meta-analytic review. *Personnel Psychology, 48*(4), 887–910.

Raffiee, J., & Coff, R. (2016). Micro-foundations of firm-specific human capital: When do employees perceive their skills to be firm-specific? *Academy of Management Journal, 59*(3), 766–790.

Rajan, R. G., & Zingales, L. (2001). The firm as a dedicated hierarchy: A theory of the origins and growth of firms. *Quarterly Journal of Economics, 116*(3), 805–851.

Rath, T., & Clifton, D. O. (2004). The power of praise and recognition. *Gallup Business Journal*, 8 July.

Reagans, R., Argote, L., & Brooks, D. (2005). Individual experience and experience working together: Predicting learning rates from knowing who knows what and knowing how to work together. *Management Science, 51*(6), 851–1013.

Rink, F., Kane, A. A., Ellemers, N., & Van der Vegt, G. (2013). Team receptivity to newcomers: Five decades of evidence and future research themes. *Academy of Management Annals, 7*(1), 247–293.

Rosen, S. (1981). The economics of superstars. *American Economic Review, 71*(5), 845–858.

Rothaermel, F. T., & Hess, A. M. (2007). Building dynamic capabilities: Innovation driven by individual-, firm-, and network-level effects. *Organization Science, 18*(6), 898–921.

Sanders, W. M. G., & Hambrick, D. C. (2007). Swinging for the fences: The effects of CEO stock options on company risk taking and performance. *Academy of Management Journal, 50*(5), 1055–1078.

Schmidt, F. L., & Hunter, J. E. (1998). The validity and utility of selection methods in personnel psychology: Practical and theoretical implications of 85 years of research findings. *Psychological Bulletin, 124*(2), 262–274.

Sconcerti, M. (2009). *Storia delle idee del calcio* [History of football tactics]. Milan: Baldini Castoldi Dalai Editore.

Sexton, T. R., & Lewis, H. F. (2003). Two-stage DEA: An application to Major League Baseball. *Journal of Productivity Analysis, 19*, 227–249.

Shamsie, J., & Mannor, M. J. (2013). Looking inside the dream team: Probing into the contributions of tacit knowledge as an organizational resource. *Organization Science, 24*(2), 513–529.

Sirmon, D. G., Gove, S., & Hitt, M. A. (2008). Resource management in dyadic competitive rivalry: The effects of resource bundling and deployment. *Academy of Management Journal, 51*(5), 919–935.

Sirmon, D. G., Hitt, M. A., & Ireland, R. D. (2007). Managing firm resources in dynamic environments to create value: Looking inside the black box. *Academy of Management Review, 32*(1), 273–292.

Sirmon, D. G., Hitt, M. A., Ireland, R. D., & Gilbert, B. A. (2011). Resource orchestration to create competitive advantage: Breadth, depth, and life cycle effects. *Journal of Management, 37*(5), 1390–1412.

Sitkin, S. B., & Pablo, A. L. (1992). Reconceptualizing the determinants of risk behavior. *Academy of Management Review, 17*(1), 9–38.

Somaya, D., Williamson, I. O., & Lorinkova, N. (2008). Gone but not lost: The different performance impacts of employee mobility between cooperators versus competitors. *Academy of Management Journal, 51*(5), 936–953.

Spearman, C. (1927). *The abilities of man.* Oxford: Macmillan.

Staw, B. M., & Hoang, H. (1995). Sunk costs in the NBA: Why draft order affects playing time and survival in professional basketball. *Administrative Science Quarterly, 40*(3), 474–494.

Swap, W., Leonard, D., Shields, M., & Abrams, L. (2001). Using mentoring and storytelling to transfer knowledge in the workplace. *Journal of Management Information Systems, 18*(1), 95–114.

Szymanski, S. (2015). *Money and football.* New York: Nation Books.

Taylor, A., & Greve, H. R. (2006). Superman or the fantastic four? Knowledge combination and experience in innovative teams. *Academy of Management Journal, 48*(4), 723–740.

Teece, D. J. (2007). Explicating dynamic capabilities: The nature and micro-foundations of (sustainable) enterprise performance. *Strategic Management Journal, 28*(13), 1319–1350.

Teece, D. J., Pisano, G., & Shuen, A. (1997 [2008]). Dynamic capabilities and strategic management. In D. J. Teece, *Technological know-how, organizational capabilities, and strategic management: Business strategy and enterprise development in competitive environments* (pp. 27–52). Singapore: World Scientific Publishing.

Tosi, H. L., Katz, J. P., & Gomez-Mejia, L. R. (1997). Disaggregating the agency contract: The effects of monitoring, incentive alignment, and term in office on agent decision making. *Academy of Management Journal, 40*(3), 584–602.

Tosi, H. L., Werner, S., Katz, J. P., & Gomez-Mejia, L. R. (2000). How much does performance matter? A meta-analysis of CEO pay studies. *Journal of Management, 26,* 301–339.

Tripsas, M., & Gavetti, G. (2000). Capabilities, cognition, and inertia: Evidence from digital imaging. *Strategic Management Journal, 21*(1011), 1147–1161.

Tzabbar, D., & Kehoe, R. R. (2014). Can opportunity emerge from disarray? An examination of exploration and exploitation following star scientist turnover. *Journal of Management, 40*(2), 449–482.

Van de Ven, A. H., & Polley, D. (1992). Learning while innovating. *Organization Science, 3*(1), 92–116.

Vassolo, R. S., Anand, J., & Folta, T. B. (2004). Non-additivity in portfolios of exploration activities: A real options-based analysis of equity alliances in biotechnology. *Strategic Management Journal, 25*(11), 1045–1061.

Wang, H. C., He, J., & Mahoney, J. T. (2009). Firm-specific knowledge resources and competitive advantage: The roles of economic- and relationship-based employee governance mechanisms. *Strategic Management Journal, 30*(12), 1265–1285.

Weick, K. E., & Roberts, K. H. (1993). Collective mind in organizations: Heedful interrelating on flight decks. *Administrative Science Quarterly, 38,* 357–381.

Wernerfelt, B. (1984). A resource-based view of the firm. *Strategic Management Journal, 5*(2), 171–180.

Wilson, K., Sin, H. P., & Conlon, D. (2010). What about the leader in leader-member exchange? The impact of resource exchanges and substitutability on the leader. *Academy of Management Review, 35*(3), 358–372.

Wolfe, R. A., Weick, K. E., Usher, J. M., Terborg, J. R., Poppo, L., Murrell, A. J., . . . Jourdan, J. S. (2005). Sport and organizational studies exploring synergy. *Journal of Management Inquiry, 29*(14), 182–210.

Woolley, A. W. (2011). Playing offense vs. defense: The effects of team strategic orientation on team process in competitive environments. *Organization Science, 22*(6), 1384–1398.

Wright, P. M., Coff, R., & Moliterno, T. P. (2014). Strategic human capital: Crossing the great divide [Editorial]. *Journal of Management* [Special Issue], *40*(2), 353–370.

Wright, P. M., & McMahan, G. C. (1992). Theoretical perspectives for strategic human resource management. *Journal of Management, 18*(2), 295–320.

Wright, P. M., & McMahan, G. C. (2011). Exploring human capital: Putting "human" back into strategic human resource management. *Human Resource Management Journal, 21*(2), 93–104.

Wright, P. M., McMahan, G. C., & McWilliams, A. (1994). Human resources and sustained competitive advantage: A resource-based perspective. *The International Journal of Human Resource Management, 5*(2), 301–326.

Youndt, M. A., & Snell, S. A. (2004). Human resource configurations, intellectual capital, and organizational performance. *Journal of Managerial Issues, 16*(3), 337–360.

Zajac, E. J., & Westphal, J. D. (1994). The costs and benefits of managerial incentives and monitoring in large U.S. corporations: When is more not better? *Strategic Management Journal*, *15*(S1), 121–142.

Zucker, L. G., & Darby, M. R. (1996). Costly information: Firm transformation, exit, or persistent failure. *American Behavioral Scientist*, *39*(8), 959–974.

Index